FOCKE-\

Fw 190

SERIES EDITOR: TONY HOLMES

PRODUCTION LINE TO FRONTLINE · 5

FOCKE-WULF

FW 190

Malcolm V Lowe

OSPREY
PUBLISHING

TITLE PAGE This line-up shot of Fw 190A-1s was almost certainly taken at Bremen. Focke-Wulf employed a number of official photographers to document their activities, and unfortunately the vast majority of the work of these unnamed professionals has been lost to posterity (*Focke-Wulf, Bremen*)

First published in Great Britain in 2003 by Osprey Publishing
Elms Court, Chapel Way, Botley, Oxford, OX2 9LP

ISBN 1 84176 438 8

Edited by Tony Holmes
Page design by Mark Holt
Scale drawings by Mark Styling
Index by Alan Rutter
Origination by Grasmere Digital Imaging, Leeds, UK
Printed by Stamford Press PTE Ltd, Singapore

03 04 05 06 07   10 9 8 7 6 5 4 3 2 1

EDITOR'S NOTE

To make this series as authoritative as possible, the Editor would be interested in hearing from any individual who may have relevant photographs, documentation or first-hand experiences relating to the legendary combat aircraft, and their crews, of the various theatres of war. Any material used will be credited to its original source. Please write to Tony Holmes at 10 Prospect Road, Sevenoaks, Kent, TN13 3UA, Great Britain, or by e-mail at:
tony.holmes@osprey-jets.freeserve.co.uk

For a catalogue of all Osprey Publishing titles please contact us at:

Osprey Direct UK, PO Box 140, Wellingborough, Northants NN8 2FA, UK
E-mail: **info@ospreydirect.co.uk**

Osprey Direct USA, c/o MBI Publishing, 729 Prospect Ave, PO Box 1, Osceola, WI 54020, USA
E-mail: **info@ospreydirectusa.com**

CONTENTS

FOREWORD

THE FOCKE-WULF Fw 190 made its operational début in July 1941, and caused considerable angst in the RAF for the next year until the arrival of the Spitfire IX redressed the balance. Like the Spitfire, the Fw 190 retained its cutting edge throughout the war by the constant updating of its engine power and its firepower, as well as a multitude of design refinements.

I first encountered an Fw 190 over France in the summer of 1943 while flying a Spitfire IX, and had a rousing to and fro with the German pilot for what seemed an age till we mutually recognised that we were in a combat stalemate situation and broke off the engagement while we had enough fuel to get home. Later in the year I flew a captured Fw 190A-4 and found it as superb as its reputation claimed it to be. Kurt Tank, who designed the Fw 190, was also a test pilot for his own creations, and this gave him a unique understanding of the flying qualities sought by pilots. At the end of the war I interrogated him, or at least that was the intention, but he rather reversed our roles with his keenness to have my views on the handling qualities of his masterpiece.

After I had flown all the great fighters of World War 2, both Allied and enemy, I was asked by the Americans to put them in order of merit with a résumé on each. My first three were the Spitfire XIV, the Fw 190D-9 and the P-51D (Mustang IV), with just a whisker of superiority separating them. All were technically superb, and all oozed elegant lethality. Although much has been written about most aspects of the Fw 190, this book will add to our knowledge by filling a specific gap in dealing with the production history of this truly great aircraft.

Captain E M 'Winkle' Brown CBE, DSC, AFC, MA, FRAeS, RN
Former Chief Naval Test Pilot at RAE Farnborough and
Commanding Officer of the Captured Enemy Aircraft Flight
Sussex, May 2002

Eric 'Winkle' Brown is seen sat in the cockpit of captured Fw 190A-4/U8 W.Nr. 147155 on 8 March 1944 at the Royal Naval Air Station at Yeovilton in Somerset. A Fieseler-built Fw 190, this aircraft landed in error at RAF West Malling in Kent during the early hours of 17 April 1943, its pilot from II./SKG 10 having become lost. Allocated the British serial PE882, the aircraft underwent considerable evaluation and examination before being handed over to the RAF's captured enemy flight, No 1426 Flt. It crashed, killing the unit's CO, in October 1944 (*Capt Eric Brown*)

INTRODUCTION

WELCOME TO THE FIFTH volume in Osprey's *Production Line to Frontline* series, this being the first to deal with a World War 2 German aircraft. A purpose of this volume will be to throw light onto the wartime construction and production of the Focke-Wulf Fw 190, a subject that has hitherto been neglected by many of those who have written about this famous aircraft.

Needing little introduction, the Fw 190 was without doubt one of the premier combat aircraft of World War 2. Built in several major production models, including the Fw 190A, F and G, and the re-engined and refined Fw 190D, the Fw 190 was to become a centrally important tool in the German war machine during World War 2. In a highly developed form it grew into the Ta 152, a potentially formidable machine that came too late to make a significant impact on the conflict.

Initially entering frontline service during the summer and autumn of 1941, the Fw 190 was to be built in very high numbers – upwards of 20,000 examples – in a multitude of locations by a number of distinct manufacturers.

The Fw 190 rightly put its creator, the Focke-Wulf Flugzeugbau GmbH of Bremen, 'on the map' as far as great aircraft companies are concerned. However, Focke-Wulf was already an established and increasingly successful organisation by the time that the first Fw 190 took to the air in June 1939. It was a company that was comparatively rich in talent and ideas, and even under the strictures and expectations imposed by the Nazi régime in Germany it achieved considerable latitude to develop its own ideas and designs.

The story of the Fw 190 has been written about many times, often with some aspects of the aircraft's history described in the minutest detail, but it is interesting to note how many sources appear reluctant to look at the actual production of this aircraft type. In basic terms, the manufacture of the Fw 190 came to include many of the big names in the Third Reich's aircraft industry, and was eventually to see the kind of scattering and dispersal that became a feature of Britain's wartime aircraft production. However, in Germany this developed on an even wider scale, and was carried out against a backdrop of a gradually worsening military situation as the Allies began to gain the upper hand while the war went on.

Added to this was the catastrophic Allied bombing of many production plants, and the parallel disruption of component manufacture, parts supply and a shortage of fuel – facts that are often neglected by historians. Indeed, the paucity of fuel did not just affect aircraft on the frontline, as erratic fuel and power production created problems for factories large and small throughout the Third Reich and occupied countries, especially as the war reached its climax. Similarly, the increasingly disrupted transportation network within Germany as a result of Allied bombing made the movement of components and completed aircraft a difficult and sometimes protracted business.

It is a point of great interest to this writer that a number of published sources have quoted exact production totals for the Fw 190. As any serious student of this aircraft type will confirm, the creation of an exact production and construction number list leading to a precise final total of Fw 190s produced is not possible. There are several reasons for this. The most obvious is the incomplete nature of contemporary documentary evidence. Simply, not all the relevant documents to allow an exact listing of all the aircraft produced survived the war, or its aftermath, or have yet come to light.

The Fw 190 was eventually built in a large number of locations by various different companies, and complete totals or construction number listings for some of these constructors are simply not available. Further, some identified blocks of construction numbers cannot be attributed to a specific manufacturer. This particular aspect of the Fw 190's story is a continuing tale. Perhaps in the future sufficient documents will be unearthed to allow a precise figure to be reached that everyone can agree on, but at present the best that can be done is a good detective job based on what evidence is available.

There are also a number of other complications to the overall picture, with the most obvious one being that Focke-Wulf and other companies involved in making and repairing Fw 190s tended to recycle older or damaged aircraft. Thus some airframes had more than one identity during their lives. Various prototypes were rebuilt several times, and some of the later war variants were constructed from recycled earlier models.

A well-known example of this is one of the comparatively small number of Fw 190s that are currently preserved around the world. A member of the National Air and Space Museum's collection of historic aircraft, Fw 190F-8 W.Nr. 931884 actually contains parts from at least one previous airframe, namely Fw 190A-7 Wk-Nr 640069. This discovery came about not as the result of post-war restoration work, but due to the aircraft being built from various components during the war – including the already-used fuselage.

The message from this point is that readers should view with some scepticism any source that claims to know exactly how many Fw 190s were actually built, without backing up the claim with a complete and verifiable list by *Werk Nummer*, version(s) and manufacturer, plus recycled aircraft, of every one of the aircraft that add up to that overall total. Any source that does not do this, while claiming to know a definite overall final total, in reality must at best be judged as a good guide, but at worst as simply giving yet another rough approximation. This book therefore does not attempt to fall into the trap of quoting a definite final total for Fw 190s produced. Instead, for the first time in a single English-language volume, an attempt has been made to illuminate what is known about the production side of the Fw 190 story, while hoping that continuing research will throw more light on the existing grey areas in the future.

ACKNOWLEDGEMENTS

As ever, it is a pleasant exercise to acknowledge friends and colleagues whose assistance and advice have been such an invaluable contribution towards the piecing together of much of the information and photographic content of this book. A number of specialists in their particular fields were especially helpful, including Robert Forsyth and Eddie J Creek of Chevron Publications, Richard L Ward, Jerry Scutts, Chris Ellis, Andrew Arthy and Mark Rolfe. Dick Ward was particularly helpful in pointing my ever-growing number of enquiries in the right directions.

Considerable assistance was rendered by my dear friend John Batchelor, whose help with information, photographs and sources was a major foundation of this work. Particular thanks also go to Derek Foley for his marvellous help with photographs and information. From amongst my local circle of aeronautical colleagues, special mention must go to Andy Sweet, whose substantial assistance and extensive knowledge of Luftwaffe matters proved particularly invaluable.

Chapter 11 of this book covers the daylight raid on Bournemouth by Fw 190s of SKG 10. The staff of the *Bournemouth Daily Echo* newspaper, particularly Archivist Scott Harrison, were extremely co-operative with my continual enquiries about this raid, and helpfully opened their extensive contemporary archive for my research. Local eye-witnesses and historians, including Denis Frank Allen, John Barker, Ron Charman, Joe Cottell, Vera Dibden, Charlie Elkins, Jimmy Martin, Ann Parnaby, Gwen Read, Norman Read, Bill Scott, Colin Taylor, Peter Wilson and Cyril Wright were also of great assistance.

Amongst my German colleagues, special thanks should go to my good friend Jürgen Schelling, whose information and contacts are particularly relevant and extensive. His checking of much of the German used in this book is also highly appreciated. Particular thanks also to Peter Pletschacher, Editor of *Flugzeug Classic* magazine, for his advice and ability to point my enquiries and research in the right direction. Much of the 'groundwork' in finding documents and other relevant information was performed by Peter Walter, who deserves special thanks.

During the preparation of this book it was particularly gratifying to meet the former Anton Flettner Flugzeugbau GmbH test pilot *Flugkapitän* Richard Perlia. Aged 97 when the Author interviewed him, his insights into the workings of the German aircraft industry in the 1930s and early 1940s gave a considerable amount of additional background and information about this specific subject, and a lot of extra leads.

In the Czech Republic, particular thanks to my dear friends Miroslav Khol and Lubomír Hodan for their help with photographs and information about the air war over the Czech lands during World War 2.

A special thanks must be made to Capt. Eric Brown, who compiled the Foreword for this book. Rightly one of Britain's most renowned pilots from World War 2 era, Capt Brown has a unique knowledge of the Fw 190, having test flown captured examples of the aircraft. He also famously interviewed Kurt Tank after the end of the war at a time when the Fw 190 was still very fresh in everyone's memory.

The work of actually writing this book took place over some two years, and during that time considerable assistance was rendered with the checking of text and facts by Lucy Maynard and my father Victor Lowe, himself an aviation historian of long-standing. Sadly a further source of inspiration and assistance in this project, my mother Carol Lowe, passed away during the preparation of this work. The book is respectfully dedicated to her, and to 'Misty' who was also lost along the way.

As always, constructive reader input on this volume would be most welcome. Comments, information, suggestions and photographs can be communicated to the Author at 20 Edwina Drive, Poole, Dorset, BH17 7JG, England.

Malcolm V Lowe
Poole, Dorset, October 2002

Author's Note

The structure of the German language is such that most if not all nouns have a gender. This is crucial in deciding within the use of the language how they and related words are spelt in given situations, depending upon agreements and declensions within individual sentences. In this book I have attempted to write the German words in their basic unagreed form, bearing in mind that the English language does not have noun genders or agreements based on such genders. I have also attempted to write plurals as they would be written in their simplest German form. It must similarly be remembered that not all German plurals end in an 's'.

With regard to nomenclature, I have used where possible the spellings and abbreviations as employed in documents of the time. Although some writers prefer to write the Focke-Wulf company name without a hyphen between the two words, the company almost always referred to itself on its own documents as Focke-Wulf (i.e., with a hyphen between the words) – and that is therefore the form that I have used here. Similarly, the German term for a manufacturer/constructor's airframe serial or construction number, *Werk Nummer* (plural, *Werk Nummern* – it is amazing how often that is spelt incorrectly in English-language published works) was often abbreviated as Werk-Nr. or simply W.Nr., and the latter is the form that I have used in this book. The term itself would sometimes also be written *Werk-Nummer* or *Werknummer*.

CHAPTER 1 DESIGNING A LEGEND

THE FOCKE-WULF Fw 190 was in operational service with the Luftwaffe for slightly less than four years, from the late summer of 1941 to VE-Day. In that time it gained considerable success and fame, and its celebrity status is certainly still alive and well today. Much is known and has been written about the Fw 190's operational career and the personalities who flew it in combat. Much less well known is the tremendous effort that went into producing the 20,000+ Fw 190s that were built in a process that started during the latter half of 1937.

At that time the Third Reich was only some four-and-a-half years old, Adolf Hitler having become Chancellor of Germany in January 1933, and the unchallenged *Führer* in August 1934. Yet the rearmament of the country under the National Socialist régime that Hitler and his cohorts established had been enormous in that comparatively short time. Clandestine rearmament had already been taking place even before Hitler's rise to power. But from 1933 onwards Germany's armed forces were completely reorganised and massively expanded – in secret at first, but eventually overtly as the military came to play a central role in the pursuance of the aims and ambitions of the Third Reich's foreign policy.

As a result of this military expansion, Germany's aircraft industry had received an enormous shot in the arm. This was a particularly welcome development, coming as it did following years of economic depression and uncertainty. Many companies such as Focke-Wulf were to benefit greatly from the sudden and expanding need for advanced military aircraft, and were to grow out of all proportion compared to their existence in the pre-Hitler years.

In April 1933 the *Reichsluftfahrtministerium* (RLM) was created. This was the government of the Third Reich's Air Ministry, and in the years that followed this body oversaw the expansion of the aircraft industry in Germany, produced overall production and delivery plans and issued specifications to the aircraft companies that reflected the perceived requirements of the Third Reich's military air arm, the Luftwaffe. Direction of the Luftwaffe was carried out through the office of the chief of the *Oberkommando der Luftwaffe* (OKL, the Luftwaffe's High Command), which was technically a part of the RLM together with the offices of the *Reichsminister der Luftfahrt* (the Third Reich's Aviation Minister). Hermann Göring was eventually to fill both posts, as the Third Reich's Aviation Minister and as the *Oberbefehlshaber der Luftwaffe* (Luftwaffe Commander-in-Chief).

However, the RLM underwent several reorganisations during its existence, which were not always for the better. The Luftwaffe itself existed in a veil of secrecy until some time after the creation of the Third Reich, the so-called '*Reichsluftwaffe* Decree' officially proclaiming the existence of the Luftwaffe not coming into effect until March 1935.

As a backdrop to these developments, important technological advances were being made from the early 1930s onwards in the design, construction and propulsion of military aircraft. Relatively low-powered braced wooden biplanes were starting to give way in a number of countries to sleek, well-armed part- or all-metal monoplane combat aircraft propelled by increasingly more powerful high-performance engines. In Germany the Luftwaffe rapidly came to enthusiastically embrace many (although it must be admitted, not all) of the technological advances that were taking place in these fields.

German aircraft companies were encouraged by most of the relevant military and government bodies that were concerned with military aircraft development and procurement within the Third Reich, to take advantage of any advances that were relevant to warplane design and construction. Nevertheless, manufacturers were not exactly encouraged to pursue competition or long-term development and experimental work if the initiative or go-ahead for this had not come from the relevant authority – a contradiction that did not help in the long-term development of some new projects or the improvement of existing designs. Similarly, the often difficult relationship between the Luftwaffe's C-in-C, Hermann Göring, and the head of military aircraft equipment and procurement, Erhard Milch, did not make for a particularly happy situation in which Germany's aircraft companies plied their trade.

Nevertheless, the far-reaching Luftwaffe requirement for a modern fighter aircraft that was drawn up in 1934 eventually led to the adoption and production of the legendary Messerschmitt Bf 109. This superb fighter at once put Germany into the front rank of military aircraft design and operation when the first examples entered Luftwaffe service in 1937. Nonetheless, within both the Luftwaffe and the RLM there was disquiet in some quarters about all the 'eggs having being put into one basket' with the emphasis been placed on but one frontline fighter type. Most rival major powers were busily developing more than one main fighter aircraft, while Germany had just the one – with the attendant danger of being left with little modern fighter cover if problems were to surface with the Bf 109.

Although the Heinkel He 112 monoplane fighter at that time existed, having lost out to the Bf 109 in the competition for the Luftwaffe's new advanced fighter, this type was displaying serious shortcomings that necessitated almost continual redesign before it finally entered production for export customers as the He 112B. It never flew in combat with the Luftwaffe, and there is speculation that the few examples that apparently entered Luftwaffe service during the Sudeten Crisis in 1938 did so only as a propaganda ploy.

At the same time, sufficiently far-sighted members of the RLM's technical department (the *Technisches Amt*, which was tasked with future combat aircraft design and specification) realised that a potential specification for a companion to or even an eventual successor for the Bf 109 programme should be at least considered. All this thinking somewhat flew in the face of those in both the RLM and other government labour and production offices, who preferred to see fewer programmes into which Germany's production capacity could be concentrated rather than more. However, in late 1937 and into 1938 this thinking crystallised into a definite specification for a fighter supplementary to the Bf 109.

The Bremen-based Focke-Wulf Flugzeugbau GmbH was invited to propose a possible design to meet this new requirement. Focke-Wulf, by that time, was growing in favour with both the RLM and the Luftwaffe, having already created a number of on-going and apparently successful programmes. The expanding company also potentially had spare production and design capacity available. Focke-Wulf's Technical Director, *Dipl.-Ing.* Kurt Tank, together with a team of experienced aeronautical designers and engineers, set about meeting the RLM's specifications. Tank's team adopted an approach completely different to that of Messerschmitt in the creation of the Bf 109.

The Focke-Wulf proposal from the start was intended to be a rugged workhorse of a combat aircraft, able to soak up punishment in combat and also capable of giving as good as it received with a creditable weapons-carrying capability. An ability to operate from rough frontline airfields, and to be serviced by groundcrews who had received the minimum of relevant instruction, were all incorporated into the Focke-Wulf proposals.

A number of powerplant options were suggested, and it was in this area that Focke-Wulf really departed from what had become established thinking in Germany for fighter aircraft propulsion. One of the proposals from Tank's team was for a radial-engined layout, utilising the new BMW 139 two-row air-cooled radial engine. The Munich-based BMW company was bench-testing early examples of this powerplant, and at 1550 hp, it appeared to offer an advantage over contemporary German in-line liquid-cooled engines.

It has become fashionable in some published sources covering the Fw 190 to suggest that Tank had a real battle on his hands to convince the RLM that this was a better alternative than a layout incorporating a liquid-cooled inline engine as fitted, for example, in the Bf 109. In reality, Tank found considerable interest in the RLM for the radial-engine alternative. It was acknowledged that at least two American companies (Curtiss and Seversky) were pursuing radial-engine fighter designs, and the Russian radial-engined Polikarpov I-16 fighter series was already successfully combat-proven in the Spanish Civil War.

The use of an air-cooled radial engine also offered the possibility of the engine taking some combat damage and still being able to function, rather than a liquid-cooled inline engine which would obviously fail very soon if its coolant lines were hit. With much of Germany's inline-engine production capacity in any case being increasingly taken up with orders for existing or recent designs, Tank's team appeared to have hit upon a good solution in selecting a new and promising radial engine for one of their design proposals.

Focke-Wulf's work was rewarded in the summer of 1938 when the RLM's interest became firmly fixed on the radial-engine proposal, and a development contract for three (later increased to four) prototypes was forthcoming. Surviving details of this contract are actually very sketchy. The new design was given the number 190 under the RLM's type numbering system that was instituted in 1933, the full official title being 8-190 (therefore, 190 was NOT a Focke-Wulf number, but an officially sanctioned designation – Focke-Wulf had previously been allocated a block of numbers from 8-189 to 8-191).

Design work at Bremen progressed rapidly, and a wooden mock-up was duly constructed, while initial work also at

Dated 18 July 1938, this was a very early drawing of the planned fuselage layout for the Fw 190V1. Of particular note in Focke-Wulf's thinking at this time were the very streamlined cockpit cover, the ducted spinner and neat installation of the BMW 139 radial engine, and the large fuel tank behind the pilot's seat (*Focke-Wulf, Bremen*)

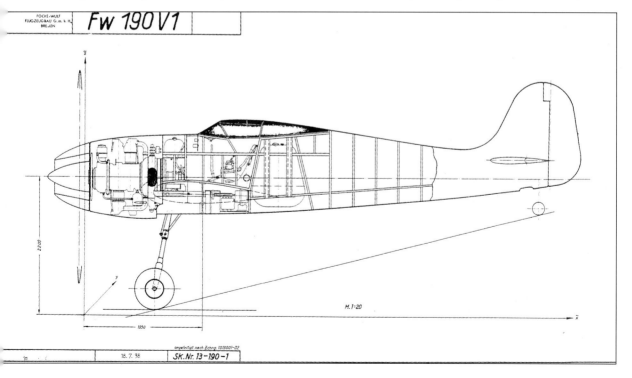

FOCKE-WULF
FLUGZEUGBAU G. m. b. H.
BREMEN

Fw 190 V1

M.1:20

18. 7. 38   *SK.Nr. 13-190-1*

angefertigt nach Zchng. 1013001-02

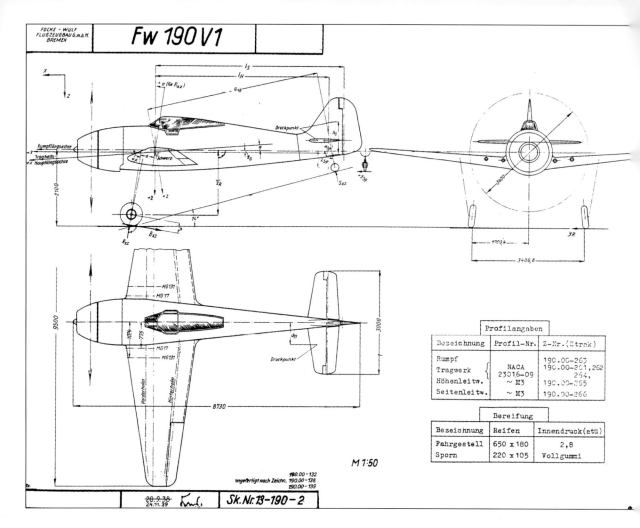

A general arrangement plan for the Fw 190V1, originally dated 28 September 1938 but later revised. Of particular note is the wing span (given at this time as 9.5 m) and the planned armament location and configuration, which on this drawing consisted of two MG 17 machine guns in the wing-roots and two MG 131 machine guns in the wings slightly outboard of these
(Focke-Wulf, Bremen)

Bremen commenced on the very first Fw 190. With the W.Nr. 0001, this first aircraft received the designation Fw 190V1, 'V' standing for *Versuchs* ('experimental', not 'prototype').

The Focke-Wulf design team had created a conventional low-wing monoplane design, with an all-metal structure and a distinctive, wide-track main undercarriage. There was ample growth potential in the original layout, and the whole structure was stressed for weights greater than those envisaged for the early aircraft. Such a design feature made it straightforward for the Fw 190 to 'grow' into the higher weights that would come when military equipment was added, and further developed versions matured.

The whole design was about as different as possible from the fighter that the Fw 190 was intended to stand alongside, the Messerschmitt Bf 109. In a piece of masterful design work, the BMW 139 radial engine was skilfully let into the aircraft's framework with a closely fitting cowling, fronted by a streamlined full-width spinner. This spinner featured a large hole in its centre to allow cooling air to reach the engine. In another respect the Fw 190 was different from its contemporaries, in having streamlined cockpit glazing faired neatly into a very low rear fuselage spine.

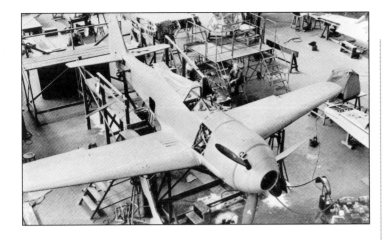

The very first of the line. This is the Fw 190V1 undergoing final assembly in the Focke-Wulf Bremen plant in the spring of 1939. The unusual ducted spinner with its large circular central intake area is particularly visible. Noticeable around the aircraft are components of another of Focke-Wulf's contemporary products, the Fw 189 twin-engine, twin-boom reconnaissance aircraft. It is possible that the aircraft (just visible) behind the Fw 190V1 could be the Fw 189V4, which approximated to the production layout of the Fw 189A production series (*Focke-Wulf, Bremen*)

This potentially gave the pilot an unrivalled view to the rear, and put the Fw 190 ahead of its time.

All of the conventional major single-seat Allied fighters of the early World War 2 period started out with a prominent, high spine behind the cockpit, thus rendering the pilot's rear view very restricted. It would be some time before such designs as the Spitfire, Mustang, Thunderbolt and others adopted the low rear spine with which the Fw 190 started life. Indeed, the Fw 190 was a world away from the ungainly, parasol wing Fw 159 which had been Focke-Wulf's previous single-seat fighter design, and which had lost out so comprehensively to the Bf 109 in the 1936 fighter selection.

Construction of the Fw 190V1 was commenced in the autumn of 1938 amid components for another of Focke-Wulf's then contemporary designs, the Fw 189 *Uhu* (Eagle Owl) twin-engine, twin-boom reconnaissance aircraft. The Fw 190V1 initially received the civil registration D-OPZE, which was later changed to FO+LY and eventually RM+CA. In keeping with the company's tradition of naming its products after birds, the Fw 190 was given the name *Würger* (Shrike, or 'butcher-bird' – the latter being a term later much over-applied to the type in the English language). The German name itself, *Würger*, actually seems to have been little used.

A front view of the Fw 190V1 at around the time of its first flight in June 1939. The distinctive full-width ducted spinner, together with an inner spinner, is especially evident. The arrangement of undercarriage doors was one of the many additional detail differences that set this aircraft apart from later production Fw 190s (*Focke-Wulf, Bremen*)

Focke-Wulf – a brief Company History

The Focke-Wulf company owes its creation to the partnership between aviation pioneers Heinrich Focke and Georg Wulf, which had started before World War I. This successful collaboration was re-established during 1921, with the creation of a two-seat monoplane called the A7 *Storch* (Stork). A tangible result of this renewed partnership was the establishment, on 1 January 1924, of the Focke-Wulf Flugzeugbau AG. Focke and Wulf received financial assistance for this venture from the Roselius family and the Bremen businessman Dr Werner Naumann. Initially, the new company's assets were the princely sum of 200,000 Reichsmarks (RM).

Focke-Wulf was established at Bremen airport, initially in premises shared with the airline Deutsche Aero Lloyd. Focke-Wulf's initial company project was the monoplane A 16 light transport, which first flew in June 1924. Over the following few years the company grew in a modest fashion with a variety of products, and in 1926 was able to establish its own facilities at Bremen airport. Sadly, Wulf was killed during 1927 while test flying one of the company's more innovative designs, the F 19 *Ente* (Duck) 'tail-first' canard monoplane.

Despite the bleak financial backdrop of the early 1930s, 1931 was a significant year for the Focke-Wulf company. In that year it absorbed the famous Albatros Flugzeugwerke GmbH of Berlin-Johannisthal, thus giving the company considerably more capacity and expansion potential. Later in 1931, a key appointment in Focke-Wulf's personnel line-up was made with the arrival from the Bayerische Flugzeugwerke AG of Kurt Tank as the new chief of the company's design and flight test departments. At this time Focke-Wulf's workforce comprised some 150 personnel, of whom some are believed to have been part-time staff.

The company continued to build competent if unspectacular production designs until the advent of the A 44 biplane two-seat trainer, which entered production as the Fw 44 *Stieglitz* (Goldfinch). This excellent design transformed Focke-Wulf into a far more important aircraft producer, and the type was also built by overseas licensees in a number of countries. Tank's personal Midas touch was by then starting to be applied to the company's designs, and the single-seat parasol-wing Fw 56 *Stößer* was the first Focke-Wulf product in which he had a major

hand. This fighter (and later advanced trainer) first flew in late 1933, and approximately 1000 were built (although some sources claim as few as 520) for home and export use.

A further major change in the company's key personnel saw Heinrich Focke leave Focke-Wulf to concentrate on rotorcraft development. The company had first become involved in this evolving method of flight through the planned licence manufacture of a Cierva autogyro design. Focke subsequently formed the Focke-Achgelis company at Delmenhorst with Gerd Achgelis to concentrate on rotary-wing craft, while Focke-Wulf itself duly concentrated only on fixed-wing aircraft.

Continuing expansion during 1936-37 occasioned the reorganisation of Focke-Wulf as a limited company with the creation of the Focke-Wulf Flugzeugbau GmbH. Control of the company passed to the German electrical firm AEG, and the company's capital balance rose in 1938 to RM 2.5 million. Part of this expansion was occasioned by Focke-Wulf starting to become involved with licence manufacture of the products of other companies. Initially this included the Heinkel He 45 biplane and the Gotha Go 145 trainer. Eventually the manufacture of both the Messerschmitt Bf 109 and Bf 110 was undertaken. This was somewhat ironic, as Focke-Wulf had lost out to Messerschmitt in the major design competition to develop a standard advanced monoplane fighter for the Luftwaffe that was won by the Bf 109. Focke-Wulf's contender had been the unusual parasol-wing retractable undercarriage Fw 159, which had eventually been beaten by the Bf 109 in the 1936 selection process that had seen the latter design carry all before it.

In fact Focke-Wulf was never to become a long-term producer of other companies products. Indeed, quite the opposite came to be the reality. By the late 1930s Focke-Wulf was gaining considerable favour with both the RLM and the Luftwaffe itself, and a number of designs that became vitally important for the company were taking shape. These included the Fw 58 *Weihe* (Harrier) twin-engined multi-purpose monoplane, the Fw 189 *Uhu* (Eagle Owl) twin-engined twin-boom reconnaissance aircraft, and the Fw 200 *Kondor*. All of these were successful designs, and the latter in particular was to put Focke-Wulf right in the centre of events. A specially equipped

Fw 200 was used by none other than Hitler himself as a personal transport at various stages in the coming years.

Yet more than anything, it was the Fw 190 that has immortalised the name of Focke-Wulf. By the time that full-scale production of the Fw 190 was being envisaged, the company had already expanded into several other premises in the Bremen area, in addition to the main plant at Bremen airport. These included Hastedt, Neuenland and Hemlingen. The company also possessed the former Albatros works at Johannisthal, and a Berlin office at Tirpitz Ufer 86-90, Berlin, W.35. The main design offices were situated at Bremen. The company's Chairman at that time was Friedrich Roselius, with Kurt Tank as Technical Director and Dr Naumann as Commercial Director.

The RLM had already developed the foresight to realise that a major conflict would probably result in considerable Allied bombing of Germany's infrastructure and industry. Plans had been discussed to disperse the German aircraft industry, and to place new factories beyond the reach of Allied bombers. The Focke-Wulf company was rather slower than most organisations to realise the considerable danger of an all-out war, even though it lay in a somewhat exposed location.

Situated as it was, close to the easy landmark of the nearby historic Hanseatic port of Bremen, Focke-

ABOVE The Focke-Wulf organisation created a string of successful aircraft programmes in the 1930s and into the 1940s that gave the company considerable prestige and financial reward. One of the important production designs for the Luftwaffe was the Fw 189 *Uhu* (Eagle Owl) twin-engine, twin-boom reconnaissance aircraft. An example of the Fw 189A design is seen here in flight over Focke-Wulf's main base at Bremen (*Focke-Wulf, Bremen*)

Wulf was potentially one of the most straightforward of Germany's main aircraft factories for Allied bombers to find, even with only basic navigational aids. Eventually, however, Focke-Wulf became one of the most dispersed of all the German aircraft companies, beginning with the establishment of a major plant at Marienburg, far to the east in Prussia.

Focke-Wulf successfully added a number of other company facilities to its inventory, including the important site at Cottbus, in eastern Germany, where production took place (amongst other locations) of the Fw 190D-9. Further plants were added at such locations as Posen, Tutow, Gdynia and Sorau. The company's design offices were eventually moved away from Bremen to a variety of other locations (although some work continued to be carried out at Bremen on a reduced scale). Much of the important design work was later carried out at the Focke-Wulf *Entwurfsbüro* (design and development office) at Bad Eilsen, near Minden, which was comparatively close to the test airfield of Langenhagen.

It was in the widespread production of the Focke-Wulf fighter by other companies that the Fw 190 has become so remarkable in the production sense. Beginning with the Fw 190A-2 onwards, a growing number of German aircraft companies became involved in its production, with Focke-Wulf being central to this eventually massive undertaking. Its importance to Germany's wartime production plans was such that a production ring was led by the company. Referred to as Production Ring F4, it consisted of Focke-Wulf at its centre, with AGO, Fieseler and Gotha as the principal constituents.

The Ring also included Aero in the Protectorate of Bohemia and Moravia, and MIAG in Germany, although these did not build Fw 190 airframes (MIAG was intended for late mark Fw 190D production, but the end of the war stopped this plan). Eventually, a very large proportion of Germany's aircraft companies were involved in the production of Fw 190s, or component manufacture, giving Focke-Wulf considerable power and influence within the industry itself. The company's workforce also expanded accordingly. It stood at 7840 in early 1938, but had grown to 28,960 by early 1944 (of the latter, 11,920 were directly involved in aircraft or component manufacture). Although exact figures are not available, this total is believed to have risen to around 38,000 by early 1945. It will be noted that many of these later employees were not of the same experienced and skilled calibre as the workforce base with which Focke-Wulf had entered the war in 1939.

The end of the war saw the disappearance of the Focke-Wulf company, but in 1951 a brand new Focke-Wulf GmbH was created, also at Bremen airport. This company eventually licence-built the Italian Piaggio P.149D trainer monoplane, and was later involved in the assembly of F-104G Starfighters for the West German Luftwaffe. The new Focke-Wulf merged with Weser ('Weserflug') in late 1963/early 1964, the original Weser company having constructed Fw 190s for Focke-Wulf during World War 2. The merger created VFW GmbH at Bremen, which amongst other products designed and built the unconventional VFW 614 short-haul twin-jet airliner.

For a time VFW partnered the Dutch company Fokker as VFW-Fokker GmbH. This partnership broke up in the early 1980s, with VFW subsequently becoming a part of MBB (Messerschmitt-Bölkow-Blohm GmbH). MBB was later absorbed by DASA (Deutsche Aerospace, also Daimler-Benz and DaimlerChrysler Aerospace), before most if not all of this organisation was amalgamated into EADS (the European Aeronautic, Defence and Space Company) in 2000. Today, the facilities at Bremen remain an important component within Europe's massive Airbus conglomerate.

On 1 June 1939, company project test pilot *Dipl.-Ing.* Hans Sander took the Fw 190V1 up from Bremen on its maiden flight. This historic first foray into the air for the Fw 190 lasted for some 30 minutes. Sander was at once impressed by the aircraft's handling qualities – a testimony to the excellent design calculations and control balancing that had been introduced into the overall design. However, on the debit side, he was almost cooked by the excessive heat in the aircraft's cockpit, which rose to around 55 degrees centigrade.

The problem was the high temperature at which the BMW 139 was running, exacerbated by the engine being situated just forward of the cockpit ahead of the firewall. Exhaust gases had also entered the cockpit due to poor sealing. Additionally, there was a problem with the main undercarriage locking mechanism. The latter was rectified comparatively easily with more positive locks, and solved altogether by the adoption on production aircraft of electric undercarriage retraction. The engine problem, however, proved rather more complicated.

EARLY TRIALS AND MODIFICATIONS

The second prototype, Fw 190V2 W.Nr. 0002 FO+LZ, first flew in late 1939. By that time the Fw 190V1 was in the hands of the *E-Stelle* at Rechlin, and considerable problems were being encountered, particularly due to engine overheating. The V2 was also fitted with the BMW 139 radial engine but eventually had a different arrangement of engine cooling that included a cooling fan in the front of the fuselage. The unusual ducted spinner of the V1 was finally abandoned as it did not give the required aerodynamic performance or cooling properties expected of it.

In January 1940 the V1 returned to the test programme fitted with a conventional propeller spinner, and a ten-blade cooling fan installed behind the spinner just ahead of the engine. The V2 was involved with initial armament trials at the test range at Tarnewitz, being the first-ever Fw 190 to be armed

Looking a little more like a production Fw 190, this is the Fw 190V1 after the removal of the original full-width ducted spinner, and its replacement with a more conventional cowling front and normal spinner. The ten-blade cooling fan for the BMW 139 radial engine is now particularly evident. Each of the three main propeller blades carried an oval decal proclaiming that it was a VDM-type propeller. The curious contraption projecting from the port wing was a probe containing various performance measuring devices *(Focke-Wulf, Bremen)*

– this armament simply comprised wing guns, as a weapons bay in the upper forward fuselage did not yet exist.

To the elation of the Focke-Wulf team that had created the Fw 190, initial official interest was sufficiently aroused by the early testing of the first two aircraft that a series of pre-production aircraft was ordered by the RLM. This was the first major step towards large-scale production of the Fw 190, with the obvious benefits that this would bestow on the Focke-Wulf company. Nevertheless, the engine problems would not go away, and indeed the whole future of the BMW 139 radial itself was by then in doubt.

The BMW company was anxious to drop this troubled engine in favour of a new 14-cylinder two-row radial, known as the BMW 801, that it had been developing from the latter half of 1938. This engine promised some 1600 hp (50 hp more than the BMW 139, with potentially further increases in power output as development continued), was likely to be less prone to overheating and would hopefully be more reliable.

To install the BMW 801 in the Fw 190 would mean a considerable redesign, however, as the new powerplant was heavier (by around 160 kg compared to the BMW 139). It was not just a case of taking out the BMW 139 and locating a BMW 801 in its place due to the relative placement of salient equipment. It must have been with some frustration that Rudi Blaser and his team returned to the drawing board and the slide rule in order to redesign the Fw 190 to accommodate the new engine.

This extremely rare view of Fw 190V5 W.Nr. 0005 shows the aircraft outside one of the Focke-Wulf hangars at Bremen in April 1940. The first Fw 190 to be powered by the BMW 801 radial engine, it embodied many of the design changes that were needed to allow the fighter to be powered by this significantly different engine. A number of Fw 189s and other aircraft can just be seen through the partially open hangar doors in the background (*Focke-Wulf, Bremen*)

The aircraft in this interesting front view is almost certainly Fw 190V5 W.Nr. 0005. The photograph clearly shows the revised undercarriage doors arrangement compared with that fitted to the Fw 190V1, and the revised cowling shape housing the 12-blade cooling fan for the BMW 801 engine. This aircraft resulted from the considerable redesign that was necessitated for the Fw 190 due to the abandoning of the BMW 139 engine that had powered both the Fw 190V1 and V2. The V5 also pioneered many of the other aspects that eventually appeared on production Fw 190s, and was instrumental in the wing design process that led to the definitive wing layout for all the production Fw 190 models
(*Focke-Wulf, Bremen*)

An immediate result was that the two final planned prototypes, the V3 and the V4, were never completed and flown. Under construction, the V3 was subsequently used for spares, while parts of the V4 were employed for static ground testing. A bill from early 1940 shows that the V3 was going to cost RM 71,940. Instead, a new aircraft, the V5 (W.Nr. 0005), had to be built from scratch to take the BMW 801.

A considerable fuselage redesign and strengthening had to take place for this aircraft, with the cockpit being moved back to balance the weight of the new engine, and a number of other major alterations being invoked. However, the rearwards-movement of the cockpit at once solved the problem of cooked pilots, as its new location was now some way behind the engine installation. This also gave sufficient room ahead of the cockpit for the addition of fuselage armament, and from thence onwards a pair of machine-guns could be fitted as required in the upper part of this newly created space.

The V5, with a pre-production BMW 801C-0 radial installed and sporting the revised fuselage, flew for the first time in April 1940. At once it became obvious that the alterations had changed the type's flying characteristics and take-off run, as well as reducing the pilot's forward view when on the ground. The wing loading had been adversely affected, and the aircraft's manoeuvrability had been accordingly degraded. Focke-Wulf's designers therefore began looking at ways to restore the commendable handling of the original V1 and V2 aircraft. This

A rear view of what is believed to be Fw 190V5 W.Nr. 0005. This aircraft began life in a dull natural metal finish, but later appears to have been painted overall RLM 02 *Grau*. This was in contrast to the V1 and V2 aircraft, which were painted in RLM 70 *Schwarzgrün*/RLM 71 *Dunkelgrün* on their uppersurfaces and RLM 65 *Hellblau* on their undersides. The Fw 190 was fitted with variable-incidence horizontal tail surfaces that the fabric-covered elevators were hinged to – this was a standard feature of production Fw 190s (*Focke-Wulf, Bremen*)

resulted in a redesign of the wing, with an increase in span as well as chord. Later, alterations were similarly made to the horizontal and vertical tail as well.

It appears that the V5 was eventually fitted with the new redesigned wing following an accident during testing. The designation V5g ('g' meaning 'großer Flügel' or big wing) has often been applied to this aircraft following modification. Certainly, Focke-Wulf drawings exist entitled 'V5g', giving a wing span with the new wing of 10,500 mm (i.e., 10.50 m), although some published sources claim that the measurement was actually 10.383 m. The V5 with the smaller wing fitted prior to these modifications is sometimes categorised in retrospect as the V5k ('k' meaning 'kleiner Flügel' or small wing).

Testing with the new wing showed that Focke-Wulf's designers had been fully successful in restoring the excellent flying and handling qualities as displayed by the first two prototypes, albeit with a slight loss of maximum speed in level flight.

The initial success of the V1 and V2 aircraft had already been confirmed by an order from the RLM for a batch of Fw 190A-0 pre-production aircraft. Some of these were already under construction, and so were finished with the original, short-span wing arrangement. It appears that 40 pre-production aircraft in total were ordered, although the actual batch of A-0s comprised 28 machines (*Werk Nummern* 0008 to 0035), with the larger wing being introduced from W.Nr. 0015 onwards. They were completed from the autumn/early winter of 1940 onwards, the first examples receiving BMW 801C-0 pre-production engines, while later machines boasted the 801C-1 radial. A 12-bladed cooling fan was fitted to most if not all of these aircraft, as used on subsequent production models.

A varied line-up of early Fw 190s in late 1940 or early 1941. The dark-coloured aircraft second from the left is the Fw 190V1 (or possibly the V2), whilst the machines on either side of it are pre-production Fw 190A-0 aircraft. The fighter third from the left has the 'long-span' wing that became standard for production aircraft (*MAP*)

Six of the A-0 machines went to the *E-Stelle* at Rechlin for service evaluation trials with the *Erprobungsstaffel* 190. Unfortunately, the early BMW 801C engines fitted to these aircraft were less than satisfactory, leading to many problems that eventually came to the attention of the RLM. The engines were prone to overheating, especially the rear row of cylinders, together with a variety of other difficulties. The BMW 801 in addition was linked to a *Kommandogerät* automatic control unit that was eventually perfected into a very successful system, but in its early days it proved highly problematical.

The whole Fw 190 programme in fact came to be in considerable trouble during the spring of 1941, and only through dedicated work by Focke-Wulf, BMW and the service test personnel at Rechlin was the Fw 190 not only kept alive but eventually passed for service introduction.

In addition to the A-0 aircraft already mentioned, sometimes similarly included in listings of the A-0 pre-production run is W.Nr. 0006, which was also used for various significant

The Fw 190A-0 pre-production aircraft W.Nr. 0006. According to some historians this aircraft did not exist, as it is not included in some published lists of Fw 190 *Werk Nummern*. However, it most certainly did exist, and it is seen here on a cold Bremen winter's day possibly just before or just after Christmas 1940. This aircraft is accepted as being known as the Fw 190V6, and it was involved in a number of development programmes, including work with the V5 on design layouts for the definitive wing planform for production Fw 190 aircraft (*Focke-Wulf, Bremen*)

An in-flight view of what appears to be Fw 190V6 W.Nr. 0006. An identifying feature of this aircraft was its straight rudder hinge line, brought about by various trials that were carried out to determine the best rudder shape and balancing. Unfortunately the wartime censor has (for some reason) retouched the cockpit area and headrest on the original print of this photograph (*Focke-Wulf, Bremen*)

The Fw 190V6 makes a run across the airfield at Bremen. Heavy exhaust staining is already marking the aircraft's fuselage, which is believed to have been painted RLM 02 *Grau* overall. Pre-production and production Fw 190s were highly prone to exhaust staining along the fuselage sides from the banks of four exhausts at the rear of the engine cowling on each fuselage side. Once in operational service, some production Fw 190s were painted with a stylised bird design on the fuselage sides that effectively covered up this staining (*Focke-Wulf, Bremen*)

trials, and a number of later development aircraft that were employed in subsequent trials and development work. Indeed, many of the Fw 190A-0 aircraft served in a wide variety of test programmes (sometimes with 'V' prefix designations applied), pioneering weapons fits, equipment placement, ground handling procedures, new engine models and the many aspects required to get a warplane ready for service use and production.

The cost of a new Fw 190A-0 with the large production-style wing was RM 152,400. In the following years, several of these aircraft were used in development programmes for later Fw 190 models, and for such work as engine trials. They also pioneered the use of factory-installed modification kits for specific versions. These were known as 'U' or *Umrüst-Bausatz* sets. The early and on-going trials of these aircraft opened the way for full-scale production of the Fw 190 to commence during 1941, and the scene was set for one of Germany's largest aircraft production programmes to get under way.

An unusual, retouched photograph of two Fw 190A-0 pre-production aircraft in flight – or possibly the same aircraft repeated twice on the same picture! The lower of the two aircraft displays clearly the ridged rudder appearance. The rudders on Fw 190s were metal framed with fabric covering *(Focke-Wulf, Bremen)*

Focke-Wulf's Winning Team

One of the great strengths of the Focke-Wulf company lay in its personnel. Central to the strong line-up of the company's skilled engineers and designers was Kurt Tank himself. Born in 1898, Kurt Waldemar Tank had seen active service during World War 1, and subsequently studied in Berlin for his engineering degree following the end of the conflict. Passing out in 1924 as a graduate engineer (*Diplom-Ingenieur*), he found employment comparatively easily in the German aircraft industry with the Rohrbach Metall Flugzeugbau GmbH.

Joining this company's design office, the young Tank participated in the design of several of Rohrbach's pioneering metal aircraft. This work culminated in the Ro IX *Rofix* single-seat fighter monoplane of 1926-27, an advanced all-metal design that pointed to Tank's growing skill and advanced thinking as an aeronautical designer. Financial problems with the Rohrbach company resulted in Tank subsequently finding employment with the Bayerische Flugzeugwerke AG, where he came into contact with another developing name in Germany's aircraft industry, Willy Messerschmitt.

While with BFW, Tank worked in the company's project office. BFW too suffered financial problems, occasioning Tank to move to Focke-Wulf in November 1931. The 33-year-old Tank became the chief of the company's design and flight test departments. This was followed two years later by his promotion to the head of Focke-Wulf's Technical Department as Technical Director. From the Fw 56 Stößer fighter design onwards, Tank played an

BELOW Kurt Tank in the cockpit of an Fw 190. Not only a talented designer, Tank was also a highly competent pilot who very often flew examples of Focke-Wulf aircraft. Nevertheless, he insisted on being regarded as a civilian pilot, even though he was apparently considered to be the chief of the factory defence flight intended to specifically defend the Focke-Wulf plant at Bremen (*Focke-Wulf, Bremen*)

important part in all of Focke-Wulf's subsequent major projects. He had learned to fly during the 1920s, and became an accomplished test pilot in addition to being a talented and innovative aircraft designer.

Tank was also a considerable motivator of those around him, and was able to spot talented designers and engineers – thus ensuring that Focke-Wulf's design team at Bremen grew to be a formidable and comparatively close-knit community whose greatest triumph was undoubtedly the Fw 190 itself. Tank's own influence and position in the company resulted in several of the later Focke-Wulf products carrying his initials in their designations, including the Ta 152 – a great honour that was rarely bestowed on German designers during World War 2. He received a Professorship during the later stages of the conflict, and ended the war in Focke-Wulf's dispersed design offices at Bad Eilsen.

Falling into British hands in April 1945, Tank was able to resume his career in the aircraft industry when the dust started to settle after the end of the war. He eventually found his way to Argentina, and was involved in the indigenous *Pulqúi II* jet fighter project, which drew on some of the aspects of the late-war Focke-Wulf Ta 183 jet fighter project.

By the late 1950s Tank was in India, where he duly collaborated with Hindustan Aircraft (later Aeronautics) Ltd in the creation of the HAL HF-24 *Marut* supersonic fighter/attack aircraft. He returned to Germany in 1968, and into retirement at the end

of a virtually life-long association with the aircraft industry. He died in June 1983 at the age of 85.

Tank was the first to admit that combat aircraft design and development is the result of team-work, and at Focke-Wulf he had a talented and dedicated team to aid him. When work began on the Fw 190 in the summer of 1938, Tank was the head of the design team, and around a dozen designers and engineers were a part of the design effort on the type. Tank's assistant Willy Käther coordinated the overall design work, with input from all members of the team. The Fw 190's basic structure, detailed design work and strength calculations were the responsibility of Rudolf Blaser's small team, while the overall project responsibility and direction was looked after by Ludwig Mittelhuber.

At first the design work on the Fw 190 was undertaken at a comparatively leisurely pace – the Fw 190 was, after all, going to supplement Messerschmitt's Bf 109, the production and early service of which were already proceeding reasonably satisfactorily. However, as the political situation in Europe began to point very definitely towards the likelihood of a major war, considerable pressure began to be put onto Focke-Wulf's designers by the RLM. Several members of the team had to work virtually night and day to move the project quickly along. Such was the pressure that Rudi Blaser became ill following the Fw 190V1's successful first flight, and he subsequently had to recuperate in a sanatorium.

Several of the early Fw 190A-0 pre-production aircraft are seen here at Bremen. All the A-0 pre-production aircraft were manufactured at Focke-Wulf's Bremen plant. The nearest aircraft, W.Nr. 0010, was fitted with a BMW 801C-1 engine, unlike the C-0 model installed in most, if not all, preceding A-0 airframes. Its engine cowling is clearly marked to signify the slightly different powerplant (*Focke-Wulf, Bremen*)

ABOVE A superbly clear photograph of one of the pre-production Fw 190A-0 aircraft on the grass at Bremen in the summer of 1941. This aircraft, like some other A-0 machines, had by this time been armed with two MG 17 machine guns in the upper forward fuselage and two similar weapons in the wing-roots, and an MG FF 20 mm cannon in each outer wing weapons station. This was exactly the weapons fit of the first production Fw 190 model, the Fw 190A-1. Many of the pre-production A-0 machines such as this one were eventually painted in an immaculate camouflage appearance that mirrored the colour scheme then about to come into widespread use on frontline Luftwaffe fighters. This was the 'mid-war' grey scheme of RLM 74 *Dunkelgrau* or *Graugrün* and RLM 75 *Grauviolett* for the uppersurfaces, and RLM 76 *Weißblau* or *Lichtblau* for the undersides and fuselage side surfaces, with a smart soft grey mottle on the fuselage sides and vertical tail (*Focke-Wulf, Bremen*)

BELOW Immaculately painted Fw 190A-0 pre-production aircraft W.Nr. 0020 KB+PV. This photograph comes from a sequence of shots that are often captioned as having been taken at Rechlin during the service trials that were performed there by six of the Fw 190A-0 pre-production models. However, it seems more likely that these photographs were actually taken at Bremen by one of Focke-Wulf's own staff photographers. The design of the apron on which the aircraft is standing looks very similar to that at Bremen, and the picture appears simply to have been taken from the top of one of the numerous hangar buildings at Focke-Wulf's plant (*Focke-Wulf, Bremen*)

ABOVE What every well-dressed Fw 190 was wearing in 1941. In an extremely well thought out procedure, every Fw 190 came supplied by Focke-Wulf with its own removable covers. These were specially designed to fit the front end of the aircraft, and even the spinner was not forgotten. Tie-downs were included to allow the covers to be attached where intended to the airframe, and the whole set could be folded up to fit neatly into a bag that was also supplied to keep the covers safe when not in use. This height of Fw 190 fashion is being modelled here by the Fw 190A-0 pre-production aircraft W.Nr. 0020 KB+PV (Focke-Wulf, Bremen)

ABOVE A further photograph of Fw 190A-0 W.Nr. 0020 KB+PV wearing its all-weather covers. These covers were a very good idea to keep out the worst of weathers, as most Fw 190s spent their lives outside except when undergoing major maintenance or being rebuilt. In practice, their use was rather compromised by operational conditions, particularly later in the war when ground crews had rather more pressing things on their minds than neatly covering up their charges (Focke-Wulf, Bremen)

RIGHT This Fw 190A-0 displays some of the distinguishing features of these pre-production aircraft. The prominent 'teardrop' bulge on the side of the engine cowling covered internal pipework for air being directed to the BMW 801 engine's supercharger. This bulge was altered on production Fw 190s to have a straight upper edge. The distinctive forward-curved panel line at the top of the engine cowling was also unique to the A-0 model, production aircraft having simpler straight panel edges. The A-0s also started life without cooling slots on the fuselage sides behind the cowling, although some later sported these when they were retrospectively fitted following their successful introduction on production aircraft
(*Focke-Wulf, Bremen*)

RIGHT A tethered Fw 190A-0 pre-production aircraft has its engine ground run and other checks made. The aircraft is being held in place under the rear fuselage by straps attached to a specially shaped concrete tie-down. The wing leading edge panel on the starboard wing by the main undercarriage leg attachment/swivel has been removed, and a variety of pipes and cables have been run up into the port main undercarriage bay. The A-0 aircraft were vitally important to the whole Fw 190 programme, and several later went on to be rebuilt as prototypes or development aircraft for subsequent trials
(*Focke-Wulf, Bremen*)

ABOVE An Fw 190A-0 pre-production aircraft is refuelled in the field using a small towed fuel tender. The legend on the fuel tank says 'Ethyl 87'. This photo was almost certainly taken at Bremen during general ground handling trials for the Fw 190. The type was comparatively easy to maintain, and full instructions on servicing and general maintenance were provided in the Aircraft Handbook that came with every example. A partial airframe overhaul was recommended after every 200 engine-running hours, and a complete overhaul after five partial overhauls – the latter had to be carried out at a maintenance depot and not at unit level (*Focke-Wulf, Bremen*)

ABOVE W.Nr. 0008 bore the four-letter fuselage code/call-sign KB+PJ, and was one of the early Fw 190A-0 pre-production aircraft that was fitted with the original, short-span wing. It is seen here undergoing trials with a mobile lifting device, which has been positioned to lift up the rear fuselage. Particularly evident in this view is the fabric covering of the rudder (*Focke-Wulf, Bremen*)

ABOVE Pre-production Fw 190A-0 SB+IA (probably W.Nr. 0021) was used for general ground handling trials and familiarisation procedures for Luftwaffe groundcrews during 1941. The Aircraft Handbook published by Focke-Wulf for Fw 190 models recommended that the aircraft's external finish should be carefully examined and cleaned on a regular basis. This included washing off any dirt with clean, lukewarm water and a non-alkali soap which should then be rinsed away. Use of solvents or fuel was forbidden for this task. The aircraft was then to be carefully wiped with sponges and rags. It is left up to the reader to imagine how often this procedure was adhered to, especially when the Germans were eventually in full retreat on the Eastern Front! Similarly, oil and engine exhaust staining like that seen on this aircraft was supposed to be removed with a detergent called Ikarol 237, although in reality it often stayed where it was (Focke-Wulf, Bremen).

ABOVE A view inside the flight hangar almost certainly at Focke-Wulf's Bremen plant. In the foreground are several pre-production Fw 190A-0 aircraft, although this view is from later in the war when some of them had been retrospectively fitted with production-standard modifications – note the cooling slots behind the cowling on the nearest aircraft, SB+IJ W.Nr. 0030. The bulge on the aircraft's wing uppersurface below the cockpit and the protruding gun barrel at the wing-root reveal that it has been retrospectively fitted with MG 151 20 mm cannons in that weapons station. The next aircraft in line is KB+PI, possibly W.Nr. 0007. Forward of this is an Fw 190A-2 that can also be seen in the photograph at the top of page 35 (Focke-Wulf, Bremen)

BELOW A close-up of the forward fuselage and weapons station on Fw 190V5 W.Nr. 0005, taken at Bremen in the spring of 1940. This was the very first Fw 190 to be fitted with a BMW 801 engine, and the first to have weapons in the upper forward fuselage. The redesign of the Fw 190's fuselage layout to accommodate the BMW 801 left enough room for the installation of two MG 17 7.9 mm machine guns. In the background just behind these guns can be seen the complete BMW 801 engine assembly, soon to be installed into this aircraft *(Focke-Wulf, Bremen)*

ABOVE Another fascinating view of the interior of the Focke-Wulf flight shed almost certainly at Bremen. In the foreground is an Fw 190A-0 pre-production aircraft, but with engine cooling slots added and MG 151 weapons in the wing-roots. The Fw 190 to the right with its rudder removed is Focke-Wulf-built Fw 190A-2 W.Nr. 120251. In the near background is an early model Messerschmitt Bf 110, Focke-Wulf building these aircraft under licence. This particular airframe appears to have been retained by Focke-Wulf for trials (and, seemingly, some liaison work), although it kept its nose guns. To the left is camouflaged Fw 200 *Kondor* NA+?V, this being a transport model with fuselage side windows. The fuselage behind the A-0 is that of an Fw 191 bomber *(Focke-Wulf, Bremen)*

BELOW LEFT Preparation work is carried out in readiness for the day's flying. These machines are all Fw 190A-0 pre-production aircraft, with BMW 801C model engines, pictured at Focke-Wulf's Bremen plant. They are easily identifiable as pre-production aircraft by their teardrop-shaped cowling bulges and the lack of fuselage cooling slots behind the exhausts – the four side exhaust pipes are readily seen on the left-hand aircraft. This machine is one of the early pre-production A-0s with the short-span wing. Such is evident by the close proximity of the main undercarriage leg to the wing leading edge *(Focke-Wulf, Bremen)*

CHAPTER 2

INTO PRODUCTION

THE INITIAL PRODUCTION model of the Fw 190 was the A-1. This basic and comparatively austere version was followed sequentially in production up to and including the Fw 190A-9. As production got underway, so continued the process of improving on the basically sound Fw 190 design layout that Tank and his design team had successfully created. The initial production model, the A-1, was built between May and October

Although probably a montage of two different photographs, this picture evocatively shows the transition from pre-production to full-scale production, and the move from testing to frontline operations. A production Fw 190A-1 or A-2 'overflies' a line-up of Fw 190A-0 pre-production aircraft, on the flight line at Bremen (*Focke-Wulf, Bremen*)

1941, with the first aircraft apparently flying in May or June 1941 – sadly, the relevant Focke-Wulf documentation to positively confirm this does not appear to have survived, leading to almost wild speculation in some published sources that the first A-1 might have flown as early as the end of 1940!

On the night of 12/13 March 1941, a mixed force of 86 Vickers Wellington and Bristol Blenheim bombers raided Bremen, with the 54-strong force of Wellingtons aiming for the main Focke-Wulf factories. They inflicted considerable damage in this, the first significant raid that the Fw 190 received on its home ground. Jig assemblies and, more significantly, part of the Bremen design offices were destroyed in this raid. By that time Focke-Wulf was busily preparing a new, dispersed factory far to the east, this being at Marienburg, in Prussia. Situated south of the present-day Gdansk, the factory was built on rolling plains well out in the countryside. The location of this factory is now named Malbork, and it is in present-day Poland.

The Marienburg facility at once assumed an increased importance following the RAF raid on Bremen, and tooling up for production of the Fw 190 there gained added momentum. Some at least of the A-1 production batch were built at this factory, although just how many of the total of 102 A-1 models it produced is not clear from surviving documents. At the same time, the Arado facility at Warnemünde and the AGO plant at Oschersleben were being eased into the Fw 190 production plans as the type's initial outside suppliers.

The Fw 190A-1 was powered by the BMW 801C-1 radial, with the now standard 12-blade cooling fan, and was armed with two MG 17 machine guns in the upper forward fuselage, two of these weapons in the wing-roots, and (in many examples) two MG FF 20 mm cannons in the outer wing armament position. The MG 17 was a small calibre weapon (7.9 mm) with unimpressive penetrating power, and had

A beautifully clear photograph of one of the early Fw 190A-1 aircraft to come off the production line. This example shows many of the features introduced with the A-1, including the wing armament of an MG 17 machine gun behind the large hole in the wing-root, an MG FF 20 mm cannon outboard, a straight top to the cowling side bulge and a straight forward edge to the main cowling access panels. It is not clear from this view if this aircraft has the panel behind the cowling without cooling slots, as the engine exhaust is already very effectively staining the fuselage sides. The photo appears to have been taken at Bremen – the design of the apron that the aircraft is standing on looks very much like that at Focke-Wulf's main plant (*Focke-Wulf, Bremen*)

A close-up view of another A-1. Note the straight edge to the main cowling access hatch, protruding wing outboard MG FF 20 mm cannon, the wing-root hole behind which nestled the rather ineffective MG 17 7.9 mm machine gun and the very noticeable upper straight edge to the cowling side bulge. This aircraft is totally lacking the engine cooling slots that would be included aft of the engine cowling panels on later production versions. The buildings in the background look unmistakably like a part of Focke-Wulf's main Bremen plant (*Focke-Wulf, Bremen*)

A smart line-up of brand new Fw 190A-1s have their engines test run in the autumn of 1941. The distinctive building in the background has been variously described by past Fw 190 writers as being at Bremen, Marienburg, Warnemünde, Rechlin and a dozen other locations! Research by the Author based on German documents suggests that this location in reality is no more sinister than Focke-Wulf's main plant at Bremen, although some of the buildings at the company's then-new facility at Marienburg were similar in appearance. The factory-applied registration/code letters on the fuselage sides were not a unit designator, and would usually have been painted out and replaced by unit-level markings when the aircraft arrived at in the frontline (*Focke-Wulf, Bremen*)

become known in some Luftwaffe circles as a 'door knocker'. The MG FF was also not wholly ideal, having a comparatively low rate of fire and muzzle velocity.

Nevertheless, it was some of these A-1 model Fw 190s that began to cause consternation to the RAF when Spitfires and other British-operated aircraft started to encounter them in numbers from the late summer and early autumn of 1941 onwards, the first aircraft having been accepted by JG 26 during July and August 1941. All was not perfect with these early Focke-Wulfs, however, and engine overheating problems, fouled spark plugs,

and other related problems kept BMW and Focke-Wulf personnel busy well into the service of the initial Fw 190 fighters.

The first Fw 190 model that was produced in significant numbers was the A-2. It is also particularly interesting for this study, as it was the first Fw 190 version that was built in important numbers by outside producers in the expanding production base for the Fw 190 line. It additionally represented the first 'up-gunning' of the Fw 190 in a continuing process that was on-going throughout the subsequent production of the various Fw 190 models. The A-2 was powered by the somewhat improved BMW 801C-2 powerplant, and was the first Fw 190 model to feature the rather harder-hitting MG 151 20 mm cannon in the wing-roots. A suitable interrupter gear was finally perfected for this weapon to allow it to fire through the arc of the Fw 190's fast-turning wide VDM propeller blades.

Production of the Fw 190A-2 included machines produced by Focke-Wulf, Arado and AGO, and took place between August 1941 and the summer of 1942. Production apparently ended in

The Fw 190A-2 production model was considerably up-gunned when compared with the A-1 thanks to the addition of synchronised MG 151 20 mm cannons in the wing-roots. This aircraft is W.Nr. 120439 (possibly RR+CM), a Focke-Wulf-built A-2, seen outside that distinctive hangar as featured in other photographs in this chapter. The aircraft prominently shows off the protruding MG 151 wing-root cannon, but does not have the outer wing MG FF cannon fitted – a not uncommon situation (*Focke-Wulf, Bremen*)

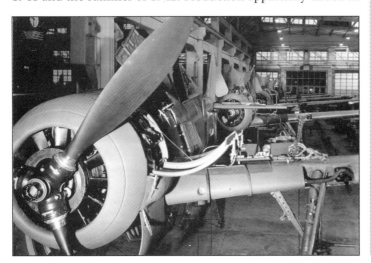

Early model Fw 190s come down the production line at Bremen, as captured by an anonymous company photographer (*Focke-Wulf, Bremen*)

ABOVE In-flight view of an early production Fw 190A series aircraft, framed through the glazing at the rear end of the fuselage nacelle of a Focke-Wulf Fw 189A twin-boom reconnaissance aircraft.

The Fw 189 was a versatile and successful aircraft that could perform a limited close support role in addition to its more normal tactical reconnaissance mission. The Fw 190 in this view has had its wing armament censored. The release-for-publication date of this photograph was 18 August 1942, but it was probably taken before that time (*Focke-Wulf, Bremen*)

LEFT An Fw 190A-2 stands in the flight hangar almost certainly at Bremen. This is the same aircraft that can be seen at the head of a line of three Fw 190s in the photographs reproduced on pages 34 and 35 in this book. In the background to the right is a Fw 191 high-altitude bomber development aircraft, a project that did not reach production status (*Focke-Wulf, Bremen*)

The neat and functional cockpit interior of an early production Fw 190, probably an A-3 version. Further details of the Fw 190's cockpit interior and an annotated interior drawing can be found on page 60 (*via J Scutts*)

July 1942 concurrently at Marienburg and Warnemünde, although the documentary evidence is very patchy from this period. The A-2 was built to the tune of at least 420 to 425 examples. Further information on this production with details of *Werk Nummer* allocations, can be found for all the production series Fw 190s in the Appendices section at the end of this book.

The Fw 190A-2 was followed by the A-3 model, which was built between February and July/August 1942 to the total of at least 580 examples (although possibly many more). The A-3 series production was significant for the introduction of a further manufacturer – Fieseler at Kassel – to add to those

A specific aerial photo sortie was flown using Fw 190A-3 W.Nr. 130471 ostensibly to create a series of photographs of the increasingly successful Fw 190 for the German press and propaganda organisations. The release-for-publication date for these pictures was 1 June 1942, but again they were probably taken before then. These photographs showed off the functional, but graceful, lines of the Fw 190, although they were retouched by the zealous German censors, including having the cockpit headrest and wing guns scratched out (*Focke-Wulf, Bremen*)

already involved in Fw 190 production. The first Fieseler-built A-3 was built in the late spring/early summer of 1942.

The A-3's armament remained similar to that of the A-2, although as with the latter, sometimes the outboard MG FF cannons were not fitted in the wings. A significant change introduced on this model was the installation of the 1700 hp BMW 801D-2 radial, which was also retrofitted to some of the previous production models. This major version of the BMW 801 represented a significant step forward, and henceforth few of the earlier problems with overheating were encountered, while the *Kommandogerät* system had also by then been perfected. Distinctive cooling slots on the fuselage sides just behind the side exhaust ports were a major distinguishing feature of Fw 190s fitted with this version of the engine. So successful was the D-2 model that it became standard for several forthcoming versions of the Fw 190A series.

By the time of the service introduction of the A-3, the Fw 190 was already being developed for fighter-bomber operations for which its speed, manoeuvrability and weapons-

Fw 190A-3 W.Nr. 130471 banks towards the camera ship to show off its wing planform during the well-known air-to-air photo sortie. This aircraft was a Focke-Wulf built-Fw 190A-3. In this view the censor has unfortunately even managed to scratch out the gun barrels of the upper forward fuselage MG 17 machine guns (*Focke-Wulf, Bremen*)

In addition to the A-0 pre-production aircraft, a significant number of production line Fw 190s were used in development work relating to the Fw 190 series, pioneering new weapons and equipment fits, and as development aircraft for later models. These were trials usually carried out by the manufacturers, or by the military test establishments of various kinds. W.Nr. 511 (as painted on the vertical tail, making it almost certainly Arado-built A-3 W.Nr. 135511) is believed to have been coded DF+GK, and amongst other trials, it was fitted with a 'tropical' filter on the side of the cowling, the ducting for the supercharger that was normally on the inside of the cowling having been opened out to an external opening to accept the filter. The aircraft also carries an ETC 501 stores rack beneath the fuselage, with stabilising fixtures for a 300-litre external fuel tank. This photograph was taken at Bremen (*Focke-Wulf, Bremen*)

carrying capacity could be fully exploited. Several A-3 aircraft were involved with the development of ground attack layouts for the Fw 190 series (in addition to other test models), and experimentation for photo-reconnaissance tasks was also being carried out. At least one A-3 was tested in the advanced wind tunnel in France at Chalais-Meudon for the aerodynamic effects of fixing attachments and hanging stores under the Fw 190. This work resulted in the short-term in the creation of fighter-bomber models within the A-series production, but in the longer-term it led to the creation of two specialised attack models of the Fw 190, the Fw 190F and G series.

By the summer of 1942, the Fw 190 was proving to be such a problem to the RAF that rather over-ambitious plans were being hatched to mount a daring commando raid across the English Channel to 'acquire' an intact example and fly it back to Britain. The arrival in error at RAF Pembrey, in south Wales, on 23 June 1942 of a pristine Fw 190A-3, together with its disorientated Luftwaffe pilot, negated the need for such a daring operation.

Believed to be Arado-built Fw 190A-3 W.Nr. 135528, this aircraft prominently displays the alternative external intake for the supercharger air ducting on the side of the engine cowling that was available for the installation of a 'tropical' filter to stop sand and dust getting into that part of the BMW 801 engine. This aircraft was possibly an A-3/U7 (*Focke-Wulf, Bremen*)

At the Sharp End

In addition to a talented collection of designers and engineers, the Focke-Wulf company also included on its books a competent flight test team. The company's pilots were kept very busy with the large amount of flight testing necessitated by the considerable number of variants, specific models, planned developments and equipment alternatives that were associated with the Fw 190 line. Rarely mentioned, but of no less importance, were the test pilots of the many other companies which also constructed Fw 190s during the war years, and the pilots of the various military test establishments – including those who tried out and qualified many of the weapons options that were a part of the Fw 190's combat capability.

As stated elsewhere, Kurt Tank himself was a very competent pilot who often test flew Fw 190 models in person (as well as flying other Focke-Wulf designs). The test pilot for the Fw 190's first ever flight, *Dipl.-Ing.* Hans Sander had joined Focke-Wulf in 1937 as a development test pilot. He led the Focke-Wulf flight test team on the Fw 190 programme (and later also for the Ta 152) as head of the company's flight test department, which was responsible for prototype flight testing of the company's new products. Born in September 1908 in Barmen (part of modern-day Wuppertal), Sander had studied car and aircraft engineering and construction at Aachen. He learned to fly during his studies, and graduated in 1934 as a *Diplom-Ingenieur*. He then studied on a three-year *Flugzeugbaumeister* aircraft construction engineering course in Berlin, a part of which was spent at Rechlin as a trainee engineering test pilot.

Graduating in 1937, Sander quickly found employment with Focke-Wulf at Bremen, and went on to work with most of Focke-Wulf's major programmes for the Luftwaffe in the following years. Although sometimes referred to as a *Flugkapitän* at

BELOW Hans Sander was rarely able to raise a smile for the camera, but he was undoubtedly one of Germany's most talented test pilots. He made the first flight of the Fw 190V1, and participated to the full in the development of the Fw 190 and its various different versions as a part of a team of talented Focke-Wulf test pilots. Many of these personnel were, like Sander, accomplished engineers as well as being gifted pilots (*Focke-Wulf, Bremen*)

the time of the Fw 190's first flight in June 1939, records appear to point to his being awarded this high-ranking civilian title in 1940. His last flight for Focke-Wulf was in April 1945, apparently at the controls of the Fw 190V73 trials aircraft.

Sander was only 37 years old when World War 2 ended. He was fortunate, like Kurt Tank, to fall into the hands of the Western Allies (and not Soviet forces) after VE-Day. Post-war, he continued his highly successful career in aviation circles, and was involved amongst other projects in the development of the F-104G Starfighter model for service in the West German Luftwaffe, for which he worked closely with Lockheed. Sander was later employed by NATO in Brussels, and made his final flight at the controls (in a glider) at the age of 72 during 1980.

Many of Focke-Wulf's test pilots have remained anonymous following the end of the war. The company employed a relatively close-knit group of test pilots, most of whom were civilians. They were overseen by an administrative team that looked after the prototype flight test programmes, kept all the paperwork up to date and were a link with the main factories and design offices. The fact that several of Focke-Wulf's test pilots were also important engineers within the company, such as Kurt Tank and Hans Sander, was a useful extra link in the chain.

A significant part of Focke-Wulf's own flight testing took place at such locations as the main site at Bremen, but also at Wenzendorf (Hamburg) and at Langenhagen just to the north of Hannover.

ABOVE Hans Sander was involved in attempts to develop a viable ejection seat system for single-seat fighters. An Fw 190A-0 development aircraft was modified for static ground ejection seat trials, but these were comparatively unsuccessful. In this view the seat has just been fired – luckily its occupant was not a real person but instead a dummy (*Focke-Wulf, Bremen*)

The Adelheide (Delmenhorst) airfield to the west of Bremen was also at times an important test site, in addition to being a significant prototype construction and conversion site. Military testing and evaluation was conducted at a variety of locations, the most important of these being the *Erprobungsstelle* (*E-Stelle*) at Rechlin. Focke-Wulf maintained an office at Rechlin to provide a link between these activities and the parent company, and to coordinate the work of the two.

The *E-Stelle* at Rechlin was officially an aviation research establishment, and was situated to the north of Berlin. It was a principal flight test establishment for new military aircraft types destined for Luftwaffe service, and contained a number of test departments that were tasked with the testing of specific equipment and its performance.

Weapons testing and qualification generally took place at official military test sites such as Tarnewitz and Karlshagen (Peenemünde), usually – but apparently not always – by military test and development pilots or seconded pilots brought in from operational units.

Significant amongst the lesser known test pilots who were on the books of the Focke-Wulf company were *Flugkapitän* Alfred Thomas, Bernhard Märschel, Werner Bartsch and the diminutive Rolf Mondry. Märschel played an important part in the development programme for both the Fw 190D-9 and the Ta 152. He performed much of the test flying, with Hans Sander, of the Fw 190 conversions that were involved in the Ta 152 development programme, as well as piloting the prototypes for the Ta 152C series.

Illustrating the dangers of flight test work, Alfred Thomas was killed in August 1944 while testing the Fw 190V30/U1 (a prototype/development aircraft in the Ta 152H programme) in a crash while trying to return to the Focke-Wulf facility at Adelheide.

Not all of Focke-Wulf's test pilots were civilians, however. A notable military test pilot who did important flight test work for the company was Oberfeldwebel Friedrich Schnier. He was involved in the test programme for the Ta 154 twin-engined nightfighter, and was seconded for work on the Ta 152 programme as well. In January 1945, flying from Focke-Wulf's flight test facility at Langenhagen in Fw 190V29/U1 W.Nr. 0054 GH+KS (the third prototype for the Ta 152H), he famously reached the exceptional altitude of 13,654 metres.

Mention must also be made of two Luftwaffe pilots who were instrumental in getting the Fw 190 qualified for military service prior to the commencement of its frontline career. Both were serving members of *Jagdgeschwader* 26, which had been earmarked as the first operational Luftwaffe unit to transition onto the Fw 190. They were Oberleutnante Otto Behrens and Karl Borris. In March 1941 they were seconded, together with Focke-Wulf technical personnel, to the *E-Stelle* at Rechlin, where six of the pre-production Fw 190A-0 aircraft had been assigned. As a part of the initial service test unit (*Erprobungsstaffel* 190), they worked hard to get the Fw 190 ready for service entry.

Things were not going at all well at that time for the Fw 190, with the engine overheating problems being a particular cause for concern. Behrens, as head of the test unit, and Borris nevertheless persevered. Their enthusiasm for the Fw 190 helped to keep the whole programme on track when it appeared to be heading for the rocks.

Kurt Tank and other members of the Fw 190 design team worked closely with Behrens to get over the potentially serious difficulties, with Tank spending much time at Rechlin. Nevertheless, an RLM team sent to Rechlin to investigate the Fw 190's problems was more inclined to have the whole programme cancelled. The excellent flying qualities of the Fw 190 – especially when flown against examples of captured Allied fighters at Rechlin – and its obvious growth potential as a high-performance weapons platform were two of its most important saving graces.

When many of the engine cooling and other difficulties had been ironed out, the Fw 190 was cleared for frontline service in July 1941. This duly allowed II.*Gruppe* of JG 26 to begin conversion to the type from the Messerschmitt Bf 109, thus commencing the Fw 190's frontline career. As for Behrens, he eventually returned to Rechlin from his service with JG 26 and remained there until the end of the war. He later followed Kurt Tank to Argentina, but was sadly killed in a crash of Tank's jet fighter creation for the Argentinians, the *Pulqúi II*.

ABOVE A close-up of what appears to be an Fw 190A-3, exhibiting a significant distinguishing feature of this version – cooling slots on the fuselage side just behind the engine cowling. Unbelievably, some published sources have claimed that these slots were exhaust outlets, which they most definitely were not. They allowed hot air from the cowling interior to escape, giving a free run of air that considerably aided engine cooling, particularly for the rear bank of cylinders on the BMW 801 engine. These slots were also retrospectively fitted to some earlier production aircraft, which might also have been re-engined with the BMW 801D series powerplant that was introduced on the Fw 190A-3 (*Focke-Wulf, Bremen*)

BUILDING THE 'ANTON'

The photographs in this chapter give a flavour of what a busy Focke-Wulf factory looked like during the production of early models of the Fw 190A. All of these images originate from the Focke-Wulf company, and were taken by staff photographers. Some are without doubt 'posed' photographs.

Those pictures amongst this selection that have been published elsewhere have been ascribed to a number of different locations. The problem with positively identifying Focke-Wulf (and indeed other company) factory interiors is that, tantalisingly, several of the company's facilities looked similar on the inside.

To add to the difficulty of identification, few drawings have ever come to light showing the architecture and structure of factory buildings of the period to positively identify specific locations. The photographs themselves are of little help. The Focke-Wulf company had a tendency of stamping the reverse side of its own works' photographs with rubber stamps that simply give a date (in some instances) and then the stock statement 'Focke-Wulf Flugzeugbau GmbH, Bremen', even if the photograph was most definitely NOT taken at Bremen!

TOP A Focke-Wulf drawing showing the basic all-metal fuselage structure of the A series, albeit in this case an Fw 190A-8 which differed (relevant to this view) from early models in the location of the access hatch on the port fuselage side aft of the cockpit, and the side panels beside the tubular engine bearers which featured neat adjustable cooling gills rather than simple cooling slots. Salient points are: 1) armoured seatback/headrest; 2) wing-root fillet; 3) armament access panel for wing-root mounted MG 151 20 mm cannon; 4) hinged side panels containing cooling gills; 5) upper forward fuselage armament access panel (*Focke-Wulf, Bremen*)

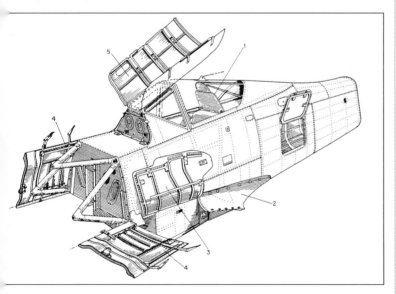

BOTTOM A Focke-Wulf drawing of the Fw 190's basic wing unit assembly. The structure was all-metal, with fabric-covered ailerons (the elevators and rudder were also fabric-covered). This is a later model Fw 190A wing, with the additional wing-root fairing (12) caused by the slightly lengthened nose of the Fw 190A-5 and subsequent Fw 190A models. Other important points are: 1) one-piece main spar; 2) rear spar; 3) wing-tips; 4) wing-root fairing; 5) removable wing leading section for main undercarriage attachment and outer wing weapons station forward access; 6) fixed leading edge; 9) wing assembly forward mounting points; 10) wing assembly rear mounting points; 11) engine lower rear support structure (*Focke-Wulf, Bremen*)

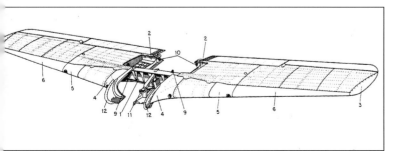

BELOW This photograph, and the following shots in this chapter, show a number of the stages involved in the construction of an early production Fw 190A. From what is known of the internal architecture of Focke-Wulf's Bremen plant, we can be as certain as is possible that all of these photographs were taken here. In this initial factory view, a complete assembly of the mid and rear fuselage is being carefully craned to the forthcoming stage in the manufacturing process *(all photographs in this chapter Focke-Wulf, Bremen)*

RIGHT A line-up of completed centre fuselage units await the addition of their vertical tails, with a line of semi-completed airframes in the background

LEFT Wing assembly underway. The section in the upper part of the photograph is the complete outer skin of the lower port wing, ready to be mated to the port wing framework below it. Note the large almost square cut-out for the outer weapons station lower access, and the smaller cut-out inboard for the ejection of spent cartridges from the wing-root weapon

ABOVE A German equivalent of 'Rosie the Riveter' and an older male colleague rivet the wing skin shown in the previous picture to the internal framework. Although the port and starboard wings were made up separately in this way, the wing final assembly was as a single unit, with the port and starboard wings mated to the one-piece main spar, as shown in the photographs overleaf

RIGHT This is what the Fw 190's wing assembly looked like when it had been put together. It was based around the one-piece main spar, which can be seen here at the rear of the main undercarriage bays. The hole in each wing-root leading edge is for the wing-root mounted weapon – either an MG 17 7.9 mm machine gun in the Fw 190A-1 or the MG 151 20 mm cannon in later models

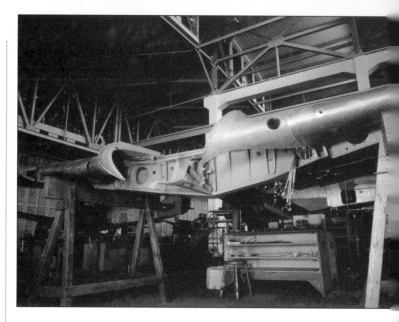

RIGHT A line-up of Fw 190 wing assemblies. This is how they came, as a single unit for attachment to the fuselage structure. Note the main spar running right the way across the span of the assembly, the main undercarriage attachment point (where the leading edge panels are yet to be fitted) and outer wing weapon station just outboard of it

RIGHT Situated beside the line of main fuselage assemblies is a line of BMW 801 power 'egg' complete assemblies, while on the other side a line of complete wing assemblies await attachment to the fuselage structures. The tubular arrangement at the front of each fuselage assembly is part of the mounting attachment (engine bearers) for the complete BMW 801 power unit

ABOVE A fantastic view inside an assembly hall at Bremen. In the foreground are two Fw 190 fuselage assemblies already mated with their vertical tails, and just ahead of them are several fuselages that have had the complete wing assembly and horizontal tail members attached. Running through the centre of the photograph are lines of separate fuselage and wing assemblies, and complete BMW 801 engine assemblies. Behind them is a further line of Fw 190 airframes coming nicely together, with a completed aircraft at its end. Situated on the far side of the hall are a number of virtually complete Fw 189As. The latter aircraft were built not only by Focke-Wulf, but mainly by other companies, including production in France

LEFT An Fw 190 fuselage is craned into place for mating with a complete wing assembly. The wing assembly has its main undercarriage attached and is essentially complete, although awaiting salient items such as the addition of its weapons. It will be noted that German aircraft factories were modern, clean, well-equipped concerns, with necessary items for mass production such as overhead moving cranes and ample work gantries for the workforce

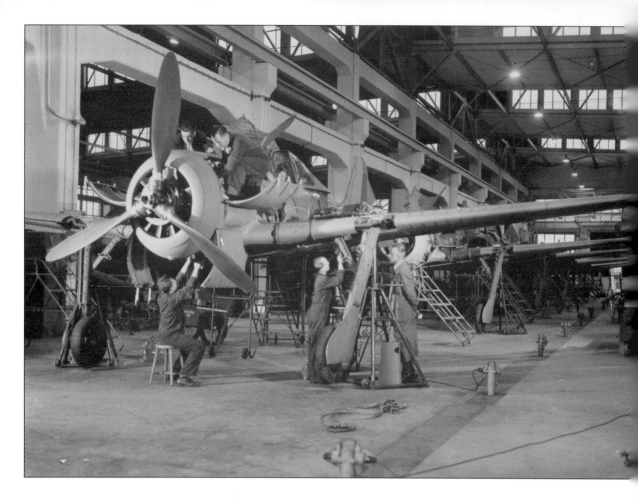

ABOVE By this stage in the production process each aircraft was coming together and looking recognisable as an Fw 190. The BMW 801 power 'egg' has been added to the forward fuselage, and everything is being wired up, connected and checked. Production workers in the German aircraft industry were well looked after, with better than average rations, good working conditions, and (at the start of World War 2) a single-shift 40-hour week. This situation gradually worsened as the war progressed, and was made more difficult with the increasing dispersion of the industry, as well as the resort to construction and sub-contraction in hastily made underground and hidden locations

BELOW The Fw 190 was a well-designed aeroplane, with good access to most of its major systems and equipment. Focke-Wulf provided excellent access to the aircraft's BMW 801 engine, incorporating large cowling panels into the design which, if necessary, could be removed altogether for maintenance

RIGHT An Fw 190 has its main undercarriage checked over by an inspector. Inspection of completed assemblies and equipment was the responsibility of the aircraft companies, overseen by inspectors from the RLM, but this theoretically effective system also tended to be degraded as production of sub-assemblies and complete aircraft was increasingly dispersed as the war went on

BELOW The starboard main undercarriage leg of an Fw 190 has its doors attached. The wing armament has yet to be fitted, while the main wheel has a typical horizontal tread pattern

ABOVE Final assembly work being performed. The main armament access panel immediately ahead of the cockpit hinged backwards over the windscreen, as shown here

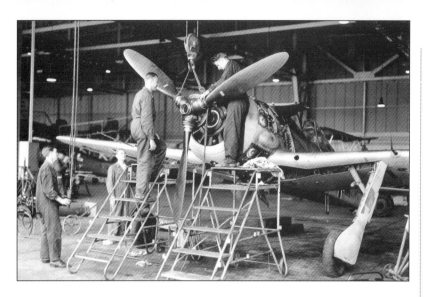

ABOVE The Fw 190's VDM propeller unit is craned into place. The aircraft in this photograph is actually one of the A-0 pre-production machines, but it effectively shows how the heavy complete propeller unit was carefully craned into place onto the engine's propeller shaft. Note once more the excellent work gantries, and the well-clothed workforce

ABOVE A young Focke-Wulf employee works on the propeller attachment of the Fw 190A-0 shown in the previous photograph. It would not have been long before he would have found himself conscripted into the armed forces, unless he sustained injury while wearing the highly inappropriate sandals that he is sporting in this view!

LEFT A completed Fw 190, with its propeller spinner attached as a finishing touch. The heavy contraption hanging from an overhead crane above the engine is the lifting device that would be used if the engine power 'egg' was going to be removed. When an engine needed to be changed, the whole unit, plus cowlings and other fittings, could be removed in one go from the Fw 190, allowing engine changes to be carried out relatively rapidly

CHAPTER 3 | IMPROVING ON SUCCESS

It was recommended that when the Fw 190 was being moved on the ground, particularly when being manhandled as in this view, there should be someone at the tail steering the aircraft with a specially provided forked detachable bar. Under no circumstances should the aircraft's control surfaces be pushed during ground handling. This Fw 190A-4 or A-5 illustrates the upright post-type attachment for the radio aerial that was introduced on the Fw 190A-4 (*via J Scutts*)

THE SUCCESSFUL INITIAL production models of the Fw 190 laid the foundations for the subsequent building of large numbers of later Fw 190As. Following on from the Fw 190A-3, the A-4 variant included a number of changes, including a revised fin shape featuring a distinctive post-type radio aerial attachment for FuG 16-type radio equipment, which replaced the FuG 7-type used previously. The A-4's armament remained similar to the A-3, although (as with the earlier models) the outboard wing MG FF cannons were sometimes omitted.

In addition to *Umrüst-Bausatz* factory kits, a variety of field-modification sets had started to become available for the Fw 190 line by this time, usually concerned with armament additions for specific tasks. These were called 'R' or *Rüstsatz* (plural *Rüstsätze*, NOT *Rüstsätzen*). Armament options for the A-4 included WGr 21 air-to-air unguided 21-cm mortar rocket equipment for attacking heavy bomber formations (Fw 190A-4/R6 model). The A-4 version as a whole also introduced several important dedicated fighter-bomber models. These included

the Fw 190A-4/U1 (some of which featured the BMW 801C-2 engine due to slow delivery of the D-2 model), the U3 (with additional armour for ground attack work, which was a forerunner of the Fw 190F-1) and the U8 (a longer-range fighter-bomber, the forerunner of the Fw 190G-1).

An underfuselage ETC 501 stores rack was usually fitted, sometimes in combination with other stores attachments. An important camera-equipped reconnaissance model, the A-4/U4, was also created. The Fw 190A-4 was manufactured from June/July 1942 until the early weeks of 1943, with just over 900 examples apparently being built. Construction was carried out by the existing team of producers.

By the time of the introduction of the A-5 model, the Fw 190 was maturing into a potent, well-armed and versatile warplane that was equally at home performing fighter, fighter-bomber or reconnaissance missions. It was capable of holding its own against just about anything that the Allies had to offer, and it was well liked by its pilots for its robustness, firepower and generally excellent handling qualities. The only obvious shortcoming was the type's comparative lack of performance at altitude, but plans were already being formulated by Focke-Wulf's busy design team to address this anomaly.

Production of the Fw 190A-5 was phased in during late 1942/early 1943, and lasted until the summer of 1943. Construction was carried out by existing manufacturers, but it additionally seems likely that the new Focke-Wulf Sorau factory might have also built A-5s. It should be noted that there were some overlaps between production of one Fw 190 model and the next. This was because not all of the various plants that were making a specific model finished production of that model at the same time, nor did they start on the next production model at exactly the same time. At least 723 A-5s were built. However, it must be pointed out that production totals for Fw 190 versions

The Fw 190 could be belly-landed with comparative success due to its configuration if flown with care and held off until a flat attitude relative to the ground could be achieved. This neatly belly-landed aircraft is TF+FM W.Nr. 665, possibly meaning 140665, which would make this a Focke-Wulf-built Fw 190A-4 (*Focke-Wulf, Bremen*)

actually become more rather than less contentious with the passage of time. There is a further discussion of this subject in the Appendices.

A significant design change that was introduced on the A-5 was a slight length increase in the forward fuselage, resulting in the engine being moved forward by 15 cm. This was to compensate for centre of gravity changes caused by increased equipment being fitted in the airframe which adversely affected the Fw 190's otherwise excellent handling. The increase changed the overall length from 8.80 m to 8.95 m (see the Appendices for more on Fw 190 dimensions, and the discrepancies between published sources on this subject).

The A-5 was also remarkable for the number of sub-variants and test aircraft that emanated from the production lines. These represented a significant effort by Focke-Wulf's designers to introduce more capabilities to the ever-growing effectiveness of the Fw 190, not just as a pure fighter but in other roles as well. The basic production aircraft retained similar armament to the previous A models, but many armament and other equipment options were pioneered by A-5 batches or individual trials aircraft, while engine development work was carried out by others. As with the A-4, several A-5 models were important in the continuing development of the type as a fighter-bomber. Significant amongst these were the A-5/U1, U3 and U8. The Fw 190A-5/U3 was the forerunner of the Fw 190F-2, while the A-5/U8 model grew into the Fw 190G-2.

Production of the Fw 190A-6 (sequentially the next production A-series version) commenced in June 1943. This model was originally devised as a heavy fighter for the Eastern Front, and manufacture was carried out by Fieseler, Arado and AGO. The A-6 introduced a considerable up-gunning of the Fw 190 line, with the addition of two MG 151 cannons in the outer wing armament position in place of the old MG FF cannons, which in any case were often not installed or removed

The Fw 190A-6 introduced a considerable up-gunning of the Fw 190A series, with the addition of an MG 151 20.mm cannon in each outer weapons station in the mid-wing location just outboard of the main undercarriage attachment. This aircraft illustrates the A-6 layout, although it is possibly an A-5/U10 development aircraft that was used as a test bed for the A-6 production version. The Focke-Wulf photograph was released for publication on 8 December 1944, but was taken well before that time (*Focke-Wulf, Bremen*)

on earlier models. The fuselage and wing-root weapons remained the same as for the A-5. To allow the fitting of the outer wing MG 151 cannons, the Fw 190's wing structure was altered and strengthened.

A number of historians claim that at this juncture, the Fw 190A's wing span was increased from 10.383 m to 10.50 m, although this is based on a misapprehension that earlier Fw 190A models had a differently sized wing (again, refer to the Appendices for more about the size of the Fw 190). Production of the A-6 model amounted to at least 569 examples and ended in late 1943, or possibly the early weeks of 1944. It was superseded by the Fw 190A-7, which had originally been intended as a dedicated reconnaissance version, and was built by AGO and Fieseler from November 1943 and Focke-Wulf themselves from December 1943.

A major development with this model was the replacement of the generally unsatisfactory upper forward fuselage-mounted MG 17 machine guns of all previous A-model aircraft with two of the much harder-hitting MG 131 machine gun of 13 mm calibre. The A-7, and subsequent models, featured a bulged gun access panel ahead of the windscreen to accommodate this larger weapon. The wing guns were standardised on four MG 151 20 mm cannons, but in the A-7 a Revi 16B gunsight was employed instead of the earlier Revi C12D.

The A-7 model was something of an interim version before the introduction of the major Fw 190A-8 model, and only 80 A-7s seem to have been made. The A-8 model represented the high-water mark of the Fw 190A series, and was built to the tune of at least 1334 examples – although again this total is open to considerable upward revision. Production was carried out at a variety of locations, including Focke-Wulf factories at Cottbus and Aslau from February 1944, Fieseler also from February 1944, AGO from April 1944, and two new players,

The Fw 190A-7 was the first variant to be fitted with two MG 131 13 mm machine guns in the upper forward fuselage weapons station ahead of the windscreen. The A-7 also featured the four wing-mounted MG 151 cannons as introduced by the Fw 190A-6, and retained the established inboard location of the pitot tube (here beside the starboard outer MG 151 cannon). The pitot fitting was moved to the wing-tip on the later Fw 190A-8. The aircraft illustrated here exactly shows these A-7 features, but it could be an A-5/U9 development aircraft that pioneered the Fw 190A-7 layout (*Focke-Wulf, Bremen*)

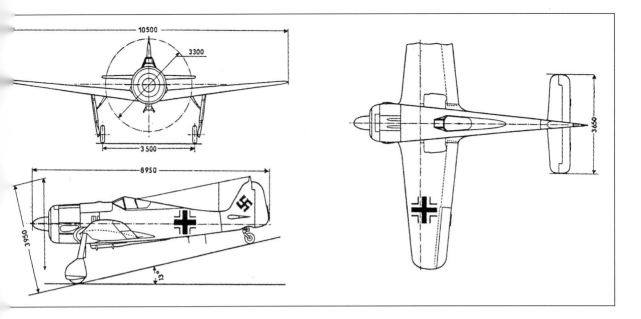

A general arrangement drawing from the Aircraft Handbook (*Flugzeug-Handbuch*) for the Fw 190A-8 (D.(*Luft*)T.2190A-8), showing the correct dimensions for the Fw 190A-8, which conflict with many subsequent published sources (*Focke-Wulf, Bremen*)

Weser and Dornier at its Norddeutsche Dornier plant at Wismar from March 1944.

The A-8's basic armament was similar to that of the A-7, but the underfuselage fittings for the ETC 501 stores rack were moved forward 20 cm. Equipment for using the WGr 21 mortar rocket (hitherto mainly available as a *Rüstsatz* add-on field installation) was built-in as standard. Also available (at least for later A-8 examples) was GM-1 nitrous oxide or MW-50 methanol-water boost for the BMW 801D-2 engine, which gave a potential improvement in performance at most altitudes. The prominent starboard wing pitot tube was moved on the A-8 to a near wing-tip location from its previous mid-wing leading-edge location. Several factories continued to produce the A-8 into 1945.

The last production model of the Fw 190A series was the A-9, which was fitted with the uprated BMW 801TS/TH engine, nominally of some 2000 hp. This was supplied (as with previous models) as a complete power 'egg', with all its fittings, and could theoretically be interchanged with the previous BMW 801D-2. It also had a larger oil cooler and oil tank, protected by a thick armoured ring ahead of the engine (previous engine models were also protected, but usually with thinner armour). Some A-9 models also sported a rounded-top cockpit canopy as fitted to a number of the dedicated ground attack Fw 190s. Some examples are known to have been fitted with a wide-chord vertical tail resembling that fitted to the Ta 152. The type's armament remained similar to the Fw 190A-8.

Production was carried out by Focke-Wulf at Cottbus, Aslau and also possibly Posen, by Arado at Tutow and Norddeutsche Dornier at Wismar. Production start-up was planned for the late autumn or early winter of 1944.

As a footnote to the story of the Fw 190A series, an A-10 model was planned, but the deteriorating war situation

Focke-Wulf's designers have rarely been given credit for the functional and well-thought-out cockpit interior design and layout of the Fw 190. In comparison to the Bf 109, the Fw 190's cockpit was much less cramped. Considerable credit for the Fw 190's interior design is attributable to Hans Sander, and the interior layout remained relatively unchanged – though not of course identical – from one version to the next. A major innovation in the Fw 190's cockpit design was the use of cockpit side consoles. Although these are now an integral part of combat aircraft cockpit interior design, and have been for many years, the Fw 190 was one of the very first major aircraft types that used side consoles in which many controls were neatly laid out and readily accessible. In the early 1940s this was a considerable innovation, most contemporary aircraft having such controls tacked onto their cockpit side walls and interior framework in a much more haphazard and untidy fashion. In this way the Fw 190's cockpit was one of the first really modern cockpit interiors. Illustrated is a typical Fw 190A-8 cockpit interior. Important points include:

1: Pilot's headset lead attachment
2: Primer fuel pump handle
3 to 6: Controls for radio set FuG 16ZY
7: Horizontal tail trim control
8: Undercarriage and flaps actuation buttons
9: Horizontal tail trim indicator
10: Undercarriage and flaps position indicators
11: Throttle (plus thumb-actuated propeller pitch control)
12: Instrument panel lighting dimmer control

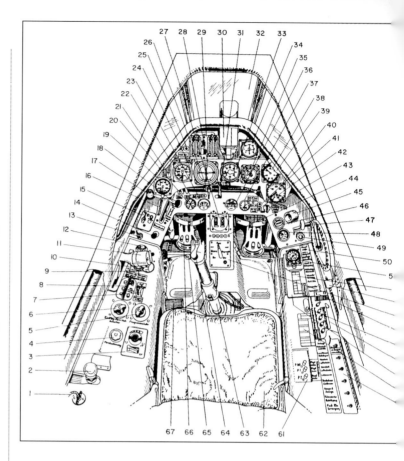

13-15: IFF control unit FuG 25
16: Undercarriage manual extension control
17: Cockpit ventilation control
18: Fuel tank selector lever
19: Altimeter
20: Fuel and oil pressure gauge
21: Pitot tube heater light
22: Manual jettison handle for underfuselage stores (when carried)
23: Oil temperature gauge
24: Air speed indicator
25-26: Armed lights check for MG 131 machine guns
27: WGr 21 mortar rocket control unit (when carried)
28: Artificial horizon
29: Armament switches, rounds counter for guns, and armament control unit
30: Revi 16B gunsight
31: Engine cooling gills adjusting lever
32: Armoured glass windscreen

33: Rate of climb/descent indicator
34: AFN-2 homing indicator FuG 16ZY
35: Compass
36: Fuel contents gauge
37: Propeller pitch indicator
38: Engine supercharger pressure gauge
39: Ultra-violet cockpit light
40: Tachometer
41: Fuel low-level warning light
42: Rear fuel tank switchover light
43: Fuel gauge selector switch
44: External load indicator lights (when carried)
45: Very pistol stowage
46: Oxygen flow/supply indicator
47: Cockpit canopy open/close actuator
48: Oxygen pressure gauge
49: Oxygen flow valve
50: Circuit breakers unit
51-52: Clock
53: Cockpit canopy jettison lever

54-55: Bomb fusing selector unit
(when carried)

56: Starter switch

57: Fuel pump circuit breakers

58-59: Compass deviation
information plate

60: Circuit breaker/fuses unit
cover plate

61: Armament circuit breakers

62: Pilot's seat

63: Control column

64: Gun/cannon trigger

65: Bomb release button (when
carried)

66: Rudder pedal with
undercarriage brakes actuator

67: Throttle lock knob

This Focke-Wulf drawing, dated
11 June 1943, shows a proposed
weapons layout for the planned
Fw 190A-10 production model.
This version, which would have
included recycled older airframes,
is not known to have been
produced. It would have included
a considerably increased outer
wing armament comprising MK
103 or MK 108 30 mm cannons
(*Focke-Wulf, Bremen*)

precluded the commencement of production. However, it is possible that some earlier models were rebuilt to approximate A-10 standard. By that time many Fw 190s were being recycled and rebuilt into other models, which considerably adds to the complication of determining how many aircraft were actually constructed from new.

The Fw 190A series spawned a number of important set-piece models and conversions. Several were used as austere nightfighters under the name *Wilde Sau* (Wild Sow/Boar). Initially, the Fw 190s involved in this project were radarless, but a number of A-6s and A-8s (and possibly A-9s) were converted into dedicated nightfighters with the installation of FFO FuG 217 or FFO/Siemens FuG 218 *Neptun* radar respectively, the latter featuring prominent drag-inducing wing-mounted aerials. Some of the converted A-8s are believed to have been fitted with the BMW 801TU engine. Similarly, the A-5 and A-8 series spawned a number of two-seat conversion trainers.

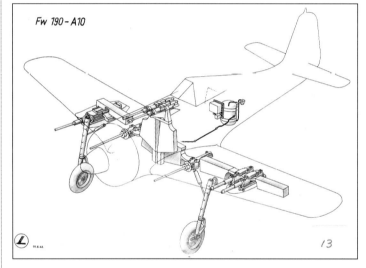

A number of two-seat conversion
trainer Fw 190s were built,
mainly, if not exclusively, by the
conversion of existing single-seat
airframes. These were mostly
former A-5 and A-8 aircraft,
although some F-8 models were
also converted. Illustrated is the
sole surviving two-seat Fw 190,
formerly Fw 190F-8 W.Nr.
584219, photographed at RAF
Chivenor in August 1972 and
now displayed at the RAF
Museum, Hendon
(*R L Ward Archive*)

Fw 190F-8 W.Nr. 584219 shows off its rather 'agricultural' cockpit architecture. Some conversions featured outward-extended glazing in the rear cockpit to increase the instructor's restricted forward view. The designations S-5 and S-8 have often been used to describe these two-seat Fw 190s, this aircraft approximating to an Fw 190S-8 or Fw 190F-8/U1 (*R L Ward Archive*)

These tandem two-seat aircraft were derived from the A-5 and A-8/U-1 series, and the designations S-5 and S-8 respectively have also been noted. The need for these aircraft stemmed partly from the increasingly large numbers of former Junkers Ju 87 pilots who were transitioning onto the attack models of the Fw 190 as the latter replaced the Stuka in some units. The exact number made is unknown, but at least one prototype conversion appears to have been constructed at Langenhagen, with others being converted at Altenburg (the home of training unit JG 110) and elsewhere, some possibly on the production line.

Much better-known are the heavily armed and armoured Fw 190s used for anti-bomber operations. These so-called *Sturm* aircraft received considerably increased add-on armour protection for the pilot and the aircraft themselves, particularly around the cockpit and cockpit glazing, and some

Fw 190s were well to the fore in the unusual *Mistel* composite aircraft programme. Photographed in May 1945 at Merseburg, this trainer *Mistel* S2 features an Fw 190A-8 as its upper component, atop Ju 88G-1 W.Nr. 590153. This was a particularly compatible combination, as the Ju 88G-1 was also powered by the BMW 801 radial engine – and, like the Fw 190, also needed a cooling fan at the front of the engines as shown here (*Robert Forsyth, Chevron Publishing*)

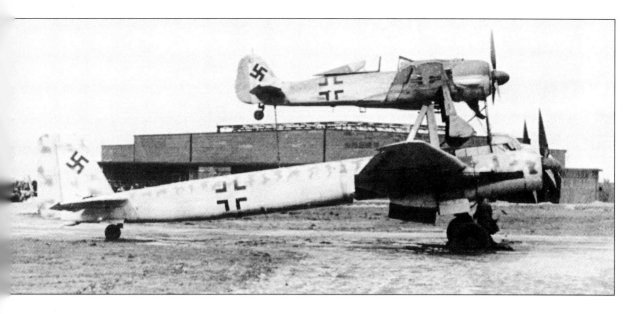

featured increased firepower with the addition of MK 108 30 mm cannons in the outer wing weapons position. Relevant conversions were made to later model Fw 190A series aircraft including examples of the A-6 and more especially the A-7 onwards.

The Fw 190 was also involved, like the Bf 109, in the unusual *Mistel* or *Beethoven* composite aircraft programme. This featured a piloted single-seat fighter being mounted on a framework above an unmanned Junkers Ju 88, the bomber being fitted with a large warhead in its nose. The manned fighter would guide the bomber towards its target and release the Ju 88 at the right moment to allow the bomber to fly into the target. The Bf 109 was initially used as the upper component of operational *Mistel* combinations when they were first used in combat in 1944, but Focke-Wulf appeared enthusiastic about joining the programme and the Fw 190 became involved later that same year. A suitable combination was the *Mistel* 2, which mated a late-mark Fw 190A with a BMW 801-powered Ju 88G-1. A number of different *Mistel* combinations were in fact either tried out or projected for the Fw 190.

Perhaps the most radical was the long-range *Führungsmaschine*, which would have mated a *Doppelreiter*-equipped Fw 190A-6 or A-8 with a specially converted Ju 88H-4. The *Doppelreiter* was a streamlined container (designed by personnel of Focke-Wulf and the Forschungsanstalt Graf Zeppelin at Stuttgartplanned) that was to be fitted onto the wing uppersurface of the Fw 190A. These containers (which in this case were to carry fuel for extending the Fw 190's range) were successfully test-flown on an Fw 190A-8 (sometimes claimed to be an A-7). Also tried out were similar containers attached to the wing underside, projecting ahead of the wing leading edges. The *Führungsmaschine* was, however, never built, neither were other *Mistel* projects such as a proposed Fw 190A-8/Ta 154A composite.

Looking ready for a test flight but actually grounded by the end of the war, this *Mistel* S3C comprises Fw 190A-8 W.Nr. 961243 above Junkers Jumo 213-powered Ju 88G-10 W.Nr. 460066 (*Robert Forsyth, Chevron Publishing*)

CHAPTER 4

FIGHTER-BOMBERS AND GROUND ATTACK

THE POTENTIAL OF THE Fw 190 for performing more than just fighter missions for air-to-air combat had been recognised from an early point in the creation of the type. Focke-Wulf's design team had built into the Fw 190's structure the strength and growth potential for it to be a versatile multi-role combat aircraft. Indeed, as previously stated, from early in the production of the Fw 190A series a number of conversions had been performed to create specific models for air-to-ground work. These had included versions with the *Umrüst-Bausatz* conversion sets U1, U3 and U8, although as the production of the Fw 190A series continued, an increasing number of combat roles and weapons possibilities were created.

The use of the Fw 190 in air-to-ground operations raised the opportunity for upgrading the Luftwaffe's attack capabilities, which had been the preserve of such types as the Henschel Hs 123 and Junkers Ju 87 during the early part of the war.

The use of the Fw 190 for missions against ground targets fell into two broad categories. These were, firstly, short-range ground attack and battlefield support operations, for which the Fw 190F series existed. Secondly, there were longer-range fighter-bomber missions for which the Fw 190G series was created. Both the F- and G-series existed alongside the main Fw 190A production series, and there were important links between them. Indeed, later in the war it was possible to find attack models of the Fw 190 that had been built using parts recycled from earlier fighter models, in addition to those put together with completely new components.

The generic term *Jabo* (short for *Jagdbomber*, or fighter-bomber) has often been used to describe these specialist attack models of the Fw 190, although the Fw 190F is better described as a *Schlachtflugzeug* (ground attack aircraft).

Work to determine air-to-ground configurations and armament for the Fw 190 had started with trials employing at least one of the original A-0 pre-production batch of Fw 190s under the designation A-0/U4. This work may have commenced as early as May 1941, and had continued with other trials of early production Fw 190s, and it eventually culminated in the adoption of the A-4 and A-5 production series for attack operations with a number of *Umrüst-Bausatz* factory conversion sets – although, due to the increased weight of the armament carried, often the outer wing MG FF cannons were removed to save weight. With the successful initial service use of the Fw 190 in air-to-ground operations, and its growing importance in this sphere of operations, Focke-Wulf began to look at putting specific attack models of the Fw 190 into production in their own right.

Initial examples of the Fw 190F had a direct link with the Fw 190 models already modified for *Jabo* operations. The F-1 in effect was created out of the Fw 190A-4/U3 version already in existence. This ground attack derivative of the standard A-4 retained the latter model's armament without the outer wing guns, and featured an ETC 501 stores carrier beneath the fuselage, able to carry a single 250- or 500-kg bomb, or four 50-kg bombs on an ER 4 rack attached to the ETC 501.

There is speculation that approximately 30 new-build F-1 models were also manufactured. The next model, the F-2, was directly linked to the Fw 190A-5/U3. This variant was redesignated Fw 190F-2, although a number of new-build F-2 aircraft were also manufactured. Production comprised some 271 aircraft built primarily by Focke-Wulf, seemingly from the Sorau factory, but AGO at Oschersleben is also believed to have been involved. Production took place between late 1942 and approximately May 1943. Modifications for operation in North Africa or the Mediterranean (or, indeed, the dusty heat of the Russian summer) were included, these comprising a

This *Schlacht* Fw 190 is believed to be an F-3/R1/tp (KO+MD?) with tropical filters attached to its cowling side supercharger air intakes, seen here at an unknown location. This aircraft is possibly an Fw 190A-5/U17, which pioneered the F-3/R1 model. Ground attack Fw 190s became very important in support of German ground forces as the war progressed (*Focke-Wulf, Bremen*)

'tropical' filter on an externally mounted air intake fitted on the engine cowling sides.

The Fw 190F-3 was the first F-series model not to be linked directly to *Jabo* modifications and conversions from the A-series production. This model was loosely based on the Fw 190A-6 in that it used the strengthened wing of the A-6, but also derived some of its features from the Fw 190A-5, including the A-5/U17 modification. This included the fitting of two ETC 50 racks beneath each wing for the carriage of 50-kg bombs (designated the Fw 190F-3/R1). In addition, a Robot-type 35 mm strike camera was often fitted inside the port wing leading edge. Between May 1943 and April 1944 this model was produced by Arado at Warnemünde, although only 530 examples appear to have been built there, possibly fewer. Like other F-series models, the F-3 had armoured (thicker) lower fuselage panels, cowling front and additional armour plating around the fuselage fuel tanks.

Although planned for production, the F-4 to F-7 models did not enter series manufacture, making the F-8 the next F-series model to see production. In fact the F-8 was arguably the most important of the F-series, and was built in large numbers. It was similar to the Fw 190A-8 model as a starting point, but aircraft of this version often carried a rounded-top cockpit canopy to improve pilot vision for close-in ground attack missions. This type of canopy was sometimes seen on other F-series aircraft.

Production of the F-8 was commenced in March 1944 by Arado at Warnemünde and by Norddeutsche Dornier at Wismar

An Arado-built Fw 190F-8/tp shows off a possible bomb load for this model of the short-range ground attack *Schlacht* Fw 190 – two ETC 50-mounted 50-kg bombs beneath each wing, and an ETC 501-mounted 500-kg bomb beneath the fuselage (R1 configuration). The machine was photographed possibly at Tarnewitz, the distinctive ground surface being a clue to this location (*Focke-Wulf, Bremen*)

What appears to be the same aircraft in the previous photograph, pictured almost certainly at the Tarnewitz weapons testing facility. The aircraft is probably W.Nr. 580383 CM+WL, a production machine that was used for a variety of weapons trials. In this view it is fitted with a single ETC 503 stores rack beneath the starboard wing
(*Focke-Wulf, Bremen*)

the following month. Also possibly involved in F-8 manufacture was AGO at Oschersleben. Many different weapons combinations were tried out on the F-8, and considerable experimentation also took place with often extraordinary concept weapons.

The type's BMW 801D-2 engine could be fitted with a supplementary fuel injection system for the short-period boost of the power available at low altitudes – many F-series aircraft spent most of their operational lives at low level. The exact number of F-8 aircraft that were built remains open to considerable debate. It is possible that the number could have been much higher than the 385 often quoted in published sources. However, figures larger than this would have contained many rebuilt and recycled airframes from other Fw 190 models. A number of examples of the F-8 were used as a part of the *Mistel* composite aircraft programme, particularly as the upper component of the *Mistel* 2 combination.

The final production example of the F-series was the F-9, although a variety of projected models were numbered after this version. The F-9 was roughly equivalent to the Fw 190A-9 (also sharing its powerplant), and had a rounded-top cockpit canopy as standard. Some examples also sported a wide-chord vertical tail resembling that fitted to the Ta 152. Production began in October 1944 and was carried out by Arado and, possibly,

Illustrative of the longer-range, fighter-bomber Fw 190G *Jabo-Rei* series is this 500-kg bomb-carrying Fw 190A-5/U8 lookalike, again probably photographed at Tarnewitz (the original print was released on 8 December 1944, but once more the picture was taken much earlier). The underwing fitment area for the large, Junkers-style fairings that mounted a 300-litre long-range fuel tank beneath each wing is visible here under the starboard wing inboard of the national insignia *Balkenkreuz* (*Focke-Wulf, Bremen*)

Dornier as a follow-on to the Fw 190F-8 manufacture. It continued until the war ended for these factories, and the total number produced is consequently unknown even to a good approximation. The F-9 introduced some alterations in the underwing and fuselage weapons racks, the common ETC 501 beneath the fuselage being replaced on some aircraft (and some F-8s) by an ETC 504, while the ETC 50 underwing racks could be replaced by the ETC 71 or ETC 503 (the latter being capable of carrying a 250-kg bomb).

The Fw 190G series existed virtually alongside the developments with the Fw 190F. However, the G-series was specifically for longer-range fighter-bomber missions compared to the F-models. This was known under the title of *Jagdbomber mit vergrößerter Reichweite*, or *Jabo-Rei* for short. As with the early models of the Fw 190F series, the early Fw 190G versions were directly linked to the fighter-bomber models of the Fw 190A-4 and A-5 series, the A-4/U8 later becoming the G-1, while the A-5/U8 was the precursor of the G-2.

Retouched but nonetheless interesting photograph of a night-capable Fw 190G-type *Jabo-Rei*. This aircraft, W.Nr. 1450 (almost certainly 151450, a Focke-Wulf-built machine), was approximate to Fw 190A-5/U2 standard, and has an anti-glare fitment above the fuselage side cooling gills to shield the exhaust glare from the pilot. Powerful lights are mounted in the port wing leading edge ahead of the long-range fuel tank, and a camera installation is just inboard of these lights. The underwing 300-litre fuel tanks are hung from simplified Messerschmitt or Focke-Wulf pylons (*Focke-Wulf, Bremen*)

The combat range of these aircraft was considerably extended through the use of 300-litre external fuel tanks beneath the wings, these being carried on a possible variety of stores racks including streamlined Junkers-type mountings or simplified pylons by Messerschmitt or Focke-Wulf (the latter being far less drag-inducing). On some models bombs could be carried beneath the wings as required. Usually these fighter-bombers dispensed with the fuselage-mounted machine-guns as well as the outer wing cannons, limiting the internal armament to wing-root mounted MG 151 20 mm cannons only. In this configuration, and with a 500-kg bomb on the centre-line underfuselage ETC 501 bomb rack and a 300-litre fuel tank beneath each wing, a range of up to approximately 1491 km could be achieved.

Just when the A-4/U8 and A-5/U8 were redesignated as the G-1 and G-2 respectively has become muddied by a number of RLM documents giving different dates for this changeover. Certainly sometime in mid-1943 appears to be a reasonable cut-off time, although other dates are possible.

In addition to the redesignated aircraft, production also took place of new-build or recycled airframes. Some 50 G-1 aircraft appear to have been built, plus an unidentified number of G-2s that could have been as high as some 468 examples, possibly even more. These were built up to the mid-summer of 1943. They were followed by the Fw 190G-3 model, which was

A well-known but nevertheless important photograph of A-5/U8 (Fw 190G-2 type, although also displaying G-3 [Fw 190A-5/U13] details) W.Nr. 636 standing in a snowstorm. The underwing 300-litre fuel tanks are hung from simplified Messerschmitt or Focke-Wulf carriers, and a 500-kg bomb is suspended from the underfuselage ETC 501 stores carrier (*Focke-Wulf, Bremen*)

the first of the G-series that did not have a direct link to the original Fw 190A series *Jabo* conversions, although it did include some features tried out on the A-5/U13 modification standard. In layout it was based on the A-6 configuration, but was a stand-alone production version, with manufacture commencing during the summer of 1943. This model included a PKS 12 autopilot and, like the G-2 model, was available for night operations with flame dampers on the visible fuselage side exhausts.

During the course of Fw 190 development, a number of specific ways of shielding the side exhausts from the pilot's view were tried out on different models when night operations were required, this being another of the many on-going development programmes that continued during the life of the aircraft. In addition, balloon cable cutters were fitted to the wing leading edges of some aircraft.

The planned G-4 to G-7 models did not reach production status, leaving the Fw 190G-8 as the last of the G-series production aircraft. Based on the layout and equipment of the Fw 190A-8, the G-8 nevertheless only carried wing-root MG 151 20 mm cannons without the A-8's fuselage-mounted MG 131 13 mm machine-guns (although the bulged gun access panel for these was usually retained). Underwing stores could be carried on ETC 50, ETC 71 or ETC 503 racks. With a 500-kg bomb beneath the fuselage, and a 300-litre external fuel tank beneath each wing, the G-8 had an impressive potential range of 1683 km at an average speed of 422.3 km/h.

Production began in September 1943 and continued until March 1944, by which time at least 146 examples had been built, although this figure is probably nearer to 800. Production was abandoned so that all efforts as far as the Fw 190 *Jabo* aircraft were concerned could be put into manufacture of the F-8, the need for G-series long-range fighter-bombers having become less pronounced due to the military situation which was going very unfavourably for the Germans on several fronts.

A further view of the Fw 190A-5/U8 or A-5/U13 whose *Werk Nummer* could well be 181636. The zealous German censor has removed the number '636' from the nose in this view (*Focke-Wulf, Bremen*)

CHAPTER 5

BMW POWER FOR THE Fw 190

AFTER A BRIEF INITIAL flirtation with the eventually abandoned BMW 139 18-cylinder two-row radial engine as mounted in the Fw 190V1 and V2, all the production models of the Fw 190A, F- and G-series and pre-production aircraft were powered by the BMW 801 14-cylinder two-row radial powerplant. The BMW 139 could actually trace its ancestry to the BMW 132 nine-cylinder single-row radial engine, which itself had a link to the American Pratt & Whitney Hornet radial engine – BMW owned licences to build Pratt & Whitney engines. The BMW 801, on the other hand, was a basically new design that eventually had a number of different applications, including the Fw 190 and some models of the Ju 88.

The BMW company could trace its ancestry very firmly back to World War 1, and it was organised in its post-war form as the Bayerische Motoren Werke AG in 1922. The company's main facilities were at München-Allach, with a production centre also at Eisenach. For a time BMW was associated with BFW as the BMW Flugmotorenbau. In similar fashion to many German companies in the aviation and armaments business, there was a huge expansion in terms of orders, and consequently of capital, workforce and facilities, following the accession to power of Hitler's National Socialists in 1933.

During 1939 BMW absorbed the Berlin (Spandau)-based Bramo engine company, which subsequently had an important effect on engine design and manufacture within BMW itself. By late 1939 the company was employing a workforce of 7825 at Munich, with 2158 at Eisenach and over 8600 at the former Bramo plants. This was to increase during the war, and BMW was not the only factory associated with the Fw 190 that eventually employed foreign workers – in this case including some unwilling ones in detachments from the Dachau Concentration Camp.

The BMW 801 radial engine that powered the Fw 190 was one of the company's principal products during World War 2, initially with assembly at the company's Munich plants but, increasingly from 1943, from production in the Berlin area as well. Needless to say, these facilities suffered attacks from Allied bombing, although production of the BMW 801 peaked

Work in progress fitting the propeller assembly onto the BMW 801C series engine of one of the Fw 190A-0 pre-production series aircraft. Fw 190s usually employed VDM-type propeller blades, with different models being used on specific versions, although all were of a somewhat wider paddle type compared to those used on many contemporary fighters. It has been claimed in some published sources that the late-war BMW 801TS series engine of the Fw 190A-9 and F-9 was turbo-supercharged, which is completely incorrect – no turbo-supercharged BMW 801 engine was ever used in production models of the Fw 190 (*Focke-Wulf, Bremen*)

in the Munich BMW plants at roughly 1000 units a month early in 1944.

The end of World War 2 saw the Eisenach facilities located in the newly created East Germany, but the Munich part of the company eventually went from strength to strength, and is now one of the world's principal companies in the automotive business. The company has also retained strong links to the aircraft industry, and in 1990 formed a joint venture with old rival Rolls-Royce as BMW Rolls-Royce GmbH.

Initial bench-testing of the BMW 801 took place during the first half of 1939, following design work which had commenced the previous year. Early results must have been very good, as the engine was rapidly cleared for series production in late 1939. The first production line models were built in mid-1940 at BMW's Munich facilities.

It has often been claimed that this production clearance was premature, and certainly the initial problems that were encountered with the BMW 801 in the early production models of the Fw 190 were a serious problem not just for the engine, but for the whole Fw 190 programme itself.

The initial model of the engine that was manufactured was the BMW 801A, but the early production models of the Fw 190

were powered by the BMW 801C series. The most numerous versions were the BMW 801D series engines that powered most of the production A-series Fw 190s and their derivatives. Throughout the war, BMW continued development work on the engine, and it eventually matured into a successful, reliable and dependable powerplant that could take considerable battle damage yet still continue running.

Eventually, there were so many BMW 801 models and projects that the company almost went through the whole alphabet, with the late-war TS/TH being the most powerful production models for the late production Fw 190A and F-series. Some of this development work concerned the quest to give the BMW 801 more respectable performance at higher altitudes, but this work was largely fruitless. This led to later developments of the Fw 190 being powered not by the BMW 801, but by a completely different engine, the inline, liquid-cooled Junkers Jumo 213.

Fully indicative of the production models of the BMW 801, the BMW 801D series engine was an air-cooled, 14-cylinder fuel-injected radial engine fitted with a two-stage supercharger and a 12-blade cooling fan. In flight, the *Kommandogerät* control system automatically controlled RPM, fuel mixture, ignition timing, the supercharger switchover control and boost pressure. This considerably reduced pilot workload and made for a smoother engine operation over a wide range of flight

Left-hand side-view illustration of a BMW 801C series engine. Note the cooling fan mounted at the front of the engine. BMW 801C series engines powered early Fw 190 models, but were replaced by the improved BMW 801D series engine from the Fw 190A-3 production model onwards. A 12-blade cooling fan was standard, except for late-war engines (for example the TS/TH series), which had a 14-blade fan (*Focke-Wulf, Bremen*)

ABOVE A BMW 801D-2 installation in an Fw 190A. The whole powerplant arrangement was neat and closely cowled, one of the finest examples of radial engine installation in a World War 2 fighter. This aircraft has 'tropical' filters to its open-fronted supercharger air intakes (the large pipe-like structure beneath the open side cowling panel (*Focke-Wulf, Bremen*)

LEFT The starboard side of the aircraft in the previous photograph. The four large pipes with oval ends are four of the engine's exhaust pipes. The framework with holes in its side aft of the engine is part of the machine-gun mounting for the upper forward fuselage weapons station. The oval shape on the side panel aft of the tubular engine bearers is a filler point for the forward fuselage fuel tank – the triangle above it states 'C3 100' referring to the type of fuel, although this was often of a lower 96/97 octane rating (*Focke-Wulf, Bremen*)

envelopes and requirements. In some cases (for example in the Fw 190F-8) a supplementary fuel injection system was installed to give short-term increases in power at low altitudes (1000 m and less).

The BMW 801D-2 delivered 1700 hp for take-off (some contemporary manuals actually state this as 1705 hp). The engine was supplied direct from the factory as a power 'egg', complete with all its fittings, cowling, etc. The weight of the whole unit was some 1342 kg. The engine's 12-blade cooling fan was made from magnesium-alloy, and was geared to turn at 1.72 times the engine speed (RPM), this being about three times the propeller's speed. The engine was lubricated with 55 litres of Intava-Rotring oil, which was housed within a ring-shaped oil tank forward of the engine, protected by the armoured forward cowling ring.

In the Fw 190A-8, two self-sealing main fuel tanks were carried in the lower fuselage in a special compartment beneath the cockpit, the forward one of 232 litres, the rearward one of 292 litres. A 300-litre external drop tank was very often carried on the Fw 190A-8 by the underfuselage ETC 501 stores rack. In addition, an auxiliary fuel tank of 115 litres could be installed as necessary behind the cockpit in a space otherwise used for the fuel tank for GM-1 nitrous oxide or MW-50 methanol-water

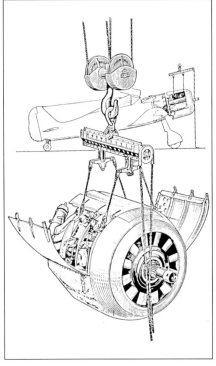

The BMW 801 was supplied as a complete engine unit with its cowling and related fitments, and was one of the first major engine types to come as a complete power 'egg' in this way. It could be hoisted into place as a complete unit by the special lifting harness illustrated, thus facilitating engine changes (*Focke-Wulf, Bremen*)

The 300-litre external fuel tank became a common fitment beneath the fuselage of Fw 190s, although several different designs of the tank itself existed. This example is shown suspended beneath an early production series Fw 190A on what was then an experimental abbreviated stores rack (*Focke-Wulf, Bremen*)

A line-up of BMW 801 engine power 'eggs' in the Focke-Wulf Bremen factory, awaiting installation. Design of the BMW 801 began in 1938 under Martin Duckstein, and the first test engine ran in May 1939. The recommended inspection cycle for the BMW 801D-2 saw a partial overhaul performed at unit level following 100 hours of operation, with a complete overhaul at a maintenance depot after every two partial overhauls (*Focke-Wulf, Bremen*)

boost for the engine when fitted. C3 petrol, nominally of 96 octane, was recommended by the manufacturer to fuel the engine.

The price in 1940 of a BMW 801A series engine was RM 80,700, and by late 1942 a new BMW 801D-2 cost RM 45,000 (of which the *Kommandogerät* was priced at RM 3000). As with production totals for the Fw 190 itself, it is impossible to say with certainty how many BMW 801 engines were manufactured.

A number of published sources have claimed around 21,000, but this would seem to be a comparatively small figure (and would assume approximately one engine for each aircraft made, which does not make sense, bearing in mind that the BMW 801 was not only used for the Fw 190). The actual figure is probably nearer to 40,000.

CHAPTER 6

PROJECTS AND FURTHER PROTOTYPES

THE LACK OF GOOD high-altitude performance from the BMW 801-powered models of the Fw 190 was a cause of particular concern for the *Technisches Amt* and the Focke-Wulf company. In reality, the BMW 801-equipped Fw 190 suffered from inadequate performance from approximately 6000 m upwards, and a number of programmes were launched by Focke-Wulf to attempt to put right this problem.

The company adopted three main approaches in an attempt to find a solution, although other potential answers were also looked at. The first approach was to develop a new Fw 190 high-altitude version based around the existing BMW 801 installation, but with the engine's power output considerably boosted and with a pressurised cockpit fitted. The second involved a re-engining of the Fw 190 with the Daimler-Benz DB 603 liquid-cooled inline engine, turbo-supercharged and again with a pressurised cabin for high-altitude operation. Thirdly, a re-engined Fw 190 powered by the Junkers Jumo 213 liquid-cooled inline engine was proposed, principally for medium-altitude combat, but still of a higher performance than the existing BMW 801-engined fighter.

The first of these three objectives developed during 1942 into the Fw 190B series, the so-called *Höhenjäger* 1. This project eventually involved a number of development aircraft, which utilised a BMW 801 engine with GM-1 nitrous oxide boosting and a pressurised cockpit.

The development in Germany of pressurisation equipment for high-altitude operation mirrored the developments also taking place at that time in Britain, but the German experiments suffered a number of problems including fractured cockpit covers. In addition, a proposed turbo-supercharger for use with the BMW 801, which would have been a further means of improving power output, was slower in development than at first envisaged. Eventually the Fw 190B series was finally abandoned, although flight trials lasted well into 1943.

The second proposal resulted during mid-1942 in what came to be called the Fw 190C or *Höhenjäger* 2 project, in which several development Fw 190s were flown with a DB 603 inline

Although this photograph has sometimes been described in publications as simply an Fw 190 cockpit, it is much more than that. It in fact shows the cockpit of one of the development high-altitude Fw 190 aircraft. Several non-standard instruments refer to pressure, and an outside temperature gauge (in the extreme top right) is also fitted, as well as additional instrumentation where the weapons status equipment would normally be found (top left) (*Focke-Wulf, Bremen*)

engine installed. The initial DB 603 conversion was made in Fw 190V13 W.Nr. 0036 SK+JS, which came from a batch of early Fw 190A airframes specifically made available for trials and development work.

Fitted with a DB 603 engine of some 1750 hp take-off power, initially without turbo-supercharging, this machine nevertheless led the way with some good performance at high altitude compared to the BMW 801-powered aircraft. A number of development C-series Fw 190s followed, one of the most important of these being Fw 190V18 W.Nr. 0040 CF+OY.

This machine was initially fitted with an unsupercharged DB 603 engine but later had an exhaust-driven turbo-super-charger installed under the designation Fw 190V18/U1. Thus converted, tests revealed that even at heights above 10,000 m, the turbo-supercharged engine could still deliver some 1600 hp, which was a major step forward in terms of engine performance and capability at altitude.

Several further development C-series aircraft followed the V18 and were numbered V29 to V33 – some of these were later to feature, much modified, in development work for the Ta 152. Fitted with a prominent under-fuselage intake for the turbo-supercharger's installation and equipment, they received the nickname *Känguruh* (Kangaroo) in some quarters.

Significant in the Fw 190C high-altitude DB 603-powered fighter programme was the development Fw 190V18 W.Nr. 0040 CF+OY. It is seen here, almost certainly amongst the factory buildings at Bremen, displaying some of the modifications for the Fw 190C programme including a pressurised cockpit with strengthened cockpit canopy, four-bladed propeller, wide-chord vertical tail and extensive external piping over the wing-roots to carry exhaust gases to the turbo-supercharger located beneath the fuselage in a large non-standard fairing (*Focke-Wulf, Bremen*)

Fw 190V18 CF+OY viewed from the rear, with the extensive piping over the wing-roots to carry exhaust gases to the turbo-supercharger being particularly evident (*Focke-Wulf, Bremen*)

In the event, the whole programme foundered on a number of technical and material problems. These included difficulties with the rudimentary pressurisation equipment, cabin sealing, cockpit canopy strength and the lack of suitable heat-resistant material for the turbo-supercharger ducting able to withstand the high exhaust temperatures that were encountered. In this latter respect, the Germans were lagging well behind the United States, where reliable turbo-superchargers were already being successfully developed.

The Focke-Wulf company is often seen as having preferred the DB 603 engine for high-altitude developments of the Fw 190, but in the event the DB 603-powered Fw 190 simply did not fulfil expectations. Instead, it was the third programme for uprating the Fw 190 (the Junkers Jumo-engined proposals) that eventually bore fruit in leading on to the Fw 190D-9 and Ta 152 production models.

Alphabetically, another missing letter in the Fw 190 production sequence additional to the failed Fw 190B and Fw 190C versions was the Fw 190E. This was originally a designation intended for a planned production series of reconnaissance models based on the Fw 190 layout. However, the reconnaissance aircraft that were derived from existing production versions such as the Fw 190A-3/U4, A-4/U4 and A-5/U4 negated the necessity for a separate Fw 190 version under the Fw 190E title.

The U4 modification set consisted of two Rb 12.5/7 x 9 cameras mounted in the lower fuselage of the fighter, plus

Although at first glance simply a photograph of a normal fighter-bomber Fw 190, this shot is in fact interesting for its background. On the far right is one of the Fw 190C high-altitude development aircraft, GH+K?, with its large underfuselage *Känguruh* fairing containing an exhaust-driven turbo-supercharger (*Focke-Wulf, Bremen*)

associated equipment and sometimes a Robot-type 35 mm camera installed inside the port wing leading edge. Other cameras, such as single Rb 20/30, 50/30 or 75/30, were also available for use.

The U4 modification proved adequate for the comparatively limited, but nonetheless important, use to which the Fw 190A was put as a reconnaissance platform. It is additionally believed that a reconnaissance model of the Fw 190D might have existed in very small numbers.

Of the many other projects that have been associated with the Fw 190, including a host of re-engined options and even a swept-wing design, mention must be made of the jet-powered design work that Focke-Wulf's designers were examining during the course of the war. Focke-Wulf in fact came up with a profusion of projects based around the then-developing advanced thinking of future jet-powered combat aircraft.

One of the earliest projects was for a jet-powered Fw 190, in which the aircraft's existing BMW 801 radial engine was proposed to be replaced by a Focke-Wulf designed turbojet. The result would have looked like an Fw 190 without a propeller. This proposal first appeared as early as 1942, but was quietly forgotten as more advanced design work on more suitable aerodynamic layouts was pursued.

Fw 190 V16 W.Nr. 0038 CF+OW was one of the initial development aircraft for the DB 603-powered Fw 190C series. Both the Fw 190B and C-series aimed at improving the Fw 190's high-altitude capability, but were ultimately unsuccessful, partly due to the Germans lagging behind in exhaust-driven turbo-supercharger technology and manufacture (*Focke-Wulf, Bremen*)

CHAPTER 7 ENTER THE 'DORA'

Smart, newly built Fw 190D-9 W.Nr. 210051 with a straight-topped cockpit cover from the first production batch of D-9 airframes. The completely changed nose contours of the Junkers Jumo 213-powered *Dora-9* compared to the BMW 801-engined Fw 190 models, plus the lengthened rear fuselage, are evident in this view *(Focke-Wulf, Bremen)*

EFFECTIVE THOUGH THE BMW-powered models of the Fw 190 undoubtedly were, the comparative lack of performance of this powerplant at higher altitudes was a problem particularly for the fighter models of the Fw 190 throughout their operational careers. As related elsewhere in this book, the Focke-Wulf company looked at various ways of addressing this problem. However, both the Fw 190B and the Fw 190C programmes that had been created to find a solution failed. Of the three main projects that Focke-Wulf had developed to address the issue of high-altitude performance, the programme that eventually bore fruit was the possibility of re-engining the Fw 190 with a Junkers Jumo 213 liquid-cooled inline engine.

Although designed as a bomber powerplant, this engine promised increased power output at altitude compared to the BMW 801 radial of the production Fw 190A and related series. It also had other potential benefits, one of which was that its design allowed the possibility of mounting a gun to fire through the propeller spinner of the aircraft – a concept already used with some success in the differently powered Bf 109. Nevertheless, the

new Focke-Wulf project to use the Junkers Jumo 213 was viewed by the company as something of a stop-gap that would perhaps hold the line until a new and better high-altitude design was brought to fruition – the Ta 152.

As it turned out, developments outside Focke-Wulf's control made the Jumo 213 powerplant readily available for fighter use. Due to the deteriorating war situation, virtually all production of piston-engined bombers was ceased in Germany during 1944 so that the German aircraft industry could concentrate on building fighters for home defence, ground attack aircraft to aid hard-pressed ground forces and jet-powered combat aircraft for a variety of defensive and offensive roles. The designation Fw 190D was given early on to the proposed Jumo 213 re-engining programme for the Fw 190, and this model was to represent the culmination of the development of the Fw 190 layout that had started life in 1938. The Ta 152, as described in the next chapter, was a very different aeroplane.

Development of the Fw 190D began in earnest during 1942, in common with the ultimately unsuccessful Fw 190B and C-series that are described earlier in this volume. In effect the new project flew in the face of one of the design factors that had been an attractive feature of the original Fw 190 layout back in 1938, in that the Fw 190 had been designed around the use of an air-cooled radial engine. Nevertheless, Kurt Tank had foreseen as early as 1941 that the mounting of a liquid-cooled inline engine in the Fw 190 could lead to major improvements in overall performance at altitude.

Originally built as an early Fw 190A-8 model at Cottbus, W.Nr. 170003 DU+JC was earmarked for development work. Heavily converted, and with its BMW 801 radial replaced by an early Junkers Jumo 213A series engine, it served as the V53 development aircraft, pioneering many production-standard modifications for the Fw 190D-9. In that form it was test flown during the summer of 1944, but still with the A-8's wing armament, which was different from the Fw 190D-9. Later, it was further altered, and was involved in weapons development work for the Ta 152B series as the Fw 190V68, for which it had a MK 103 30 mm cannon mounted in each wing-root. This photograph is believed to show the aircraft in its later configuration (*Focke-Wulf, Bremen*)

Focke-Wulf received a contract in October 1942 from the RLM for a fuselage mock-up to be made of a Jumo 213-engined layout for a future production Fw 190. By the end of 1942 at least one Fw 190, V17 W.Nr. 0039 CF+OX, was flying with a Jumo 213 installed. Just exactly when this aircraft first flew with the Jumo 213 has never been positively identified, although a number of possible dates have been named over the years. This aircraft nevertheless can be regarded as the first prototype for the Jumo 213-engined Fw 190, and it was followed by a number of other development aircraft also equipped with the Jumo 213, some of them featuring cockpit pressurisation.

However, problems were encountered with the pressurisation of these aircraft in the same way that the Fw 190B and C-series also ran into trouble. In the event, plans for a pressurised Jumo-engined Fw 190 had to be abandoned, resulting in major changes being made to the original production plans for the intended Fw 190D series.

The planned initial unpressurised Fw 190D-1 and pressurised D-2 production models were withdrawn altogether, and in the event the first model of the Fw 190D to reach production status was the unpressurised Fw 190D-9. Despite the overall pressurisation difficulties, in contrast the Jumo 213 engine had shown considerable promise when mated to the Fw 190 airframe, and was giving good performance results in test flights at up to around 6000 m – better performance in fact than was shown by the existing BMW 801-powered Fw 190 production models. In addition, this engine did not suffer from the setbacks with exhaust-driven turbo-supercharging that had beset the DB 603-powered Fw 190C-series experimental models, as it was fitted with a much more straightforward supercharger system.

Production of the Jumo 213 began in large quantities for the Fw 190D-9 during 1944, and in total almost 9200 Jumo 213 of all types were manufactured by several factories (including Dessau, Köthen, Leipzig and Magdeburg) from 1942 until war's end.

In order to make the much longer Jumo 213 engine fit into the Fw 190's layout, the nose of the aircraft had to be extended, with a consequent extension also of the rear fuselage (by use of a 50-cm extra section ahead of the tail) to retain the balance and aerodynamic qualities of the basic Fw 190 design. Once more, Focke-Wulf's designers achieved an excellent design fix that mated the Jumo engine to the Fw 190 with the minimum of major alteration, while also creating a commendable aerodynamic efficiency for the whole installation.

With the addition of an annular radiator at the front of the engine installation, the new model of the Fw 190 still looked like a radial-engined aircraft, and the whole layout was achieved with the possibility of mounting two machine-guns in the upper forward fuselage in similar fashion to the radial-engined Fw 190 models. Altogether, the fuselage length for the Fw 190D-9 was increased to 10.192 m. As the wing and centre fuselage remained

The forward end of what appears to be an experimental/development Junkers Jumo 213 engine installation layout. The Jumo 213A-1 powered the Fw 190D-9, with later Jumo 213 models being installed in the D-10 to D-13 versions. The Fw 190D-9 employed a three-blade Junkers airscrew, rather than the VDM-type units on BMW 801-powered models. Particularly evident in this view is the circular (annular) radiator typical of the Jumo 213 engine installation, which gave the appearance of a radial engine, even though the Jumo 213 was an inline engine (*Focke-Wulf, Bremen*)

essentially similar to the previous models of the Fw 190 – including the Fw 190A-8, on which structurally the D-9 was largely based – the wingspan was unchanged at 10.50 m.

During the early months of 1944 Focke-Wulf's designers worked hard on perfecting the design and creating production drawings for the Fw 190D-9 model. Rudolf Blaser, whose health had already suffered during the period of high activity when the original Fw 190V1 was being created, was also well to the fore in the effort for the D-9 model.

In addition to the various prototype/development Fw 190s that tested the Jumo 213 installation and performance, two further *Versuchs* Fw 190s were highly important in the Fw 190D-9 development. These were V53 W.Nr. 170003 and V54 W.Nr. 174024. Both were former Fw 190A-8 airframes that were brought into the D-9 test programme, and they helped to perfect the final production form for the Fw 190D-9.

The first flight dates for these two aircraft are so far unknown. However, they were involved in flight testing during the summer of 1944, and possibly first flew some time before this.

Production of the Fw 190D-9, or *Dora-9* as it is often popularly known, commenced in the summer of 1944 at Fockc-Wulf's Cottbus facility. Also eventually involved in D-9 production were Fieseler, Mimetall and possibly Norddeutsche Dornier. Initial production aircraft were completed in August/ September 1944. Production of early examples is sometimes also ascribed to Focke-Wulf at Langenhagen, and it is possible that the latter location (which, as described elsewhere, was an important flight test centre for Focke-Wulf) was involved in recycling Fw 190A-8 airframes into D-9 configuration.

Certainly, by that time, a considerable amount of rebuilding or recycling of old Fw 190s into newer models was taking place. A-8 fuselages rebuilt into D-9 configuration needed the rear fuselage extension adding, plus reinforcing strips at their front ends below and ahead of the cockpit, and a variety of other changes including new engine mounts and fittings.

In its basic production form, the Fw 190D-9 was powered by a Junkers Jumo 213A-1 12-cylinder inverted-vee inline engine of 1770 hp (although many published sources state between 1750 hp and 1776 hp), but which could still give a very useful 1600 hp at almost 6000 m. Its output could be increased to at least 2100 hp by means of MW-50 methanol-water boost in many of the D-9s that were built. Standard armament consisted of two MG 131 13 mm machine-guns in the upper forward fuselage and two 20 mm MG 151 cannons in the wing-roots. An ETC 501 or more usually ETC 504 stores carrier could be fitted beneath the fuselage as required. A rounded-top cockpit canopy was fitted to many production aircraft.

To begin with, some Luftwaffe pilots were highly sceptical of the *Dora-9* when it first entered service – especially as it was powered by an engine originally intended for bombers, and had even been admitted by Kurt Tank himself as being little more than a stop-gap measure. In reality the excellent flying qualities and performance of the Fw 190D-9 particularly at higher altitudes were soon highly appreciated. It gave the Luftwaffe's *Jagdflieger* a fighter that was at least on a par in many respects with contemporary Allied fighters such as the P-51D Mustang.

Compared to the earlier Fw 190 models, pilots found the *Dora-9* was faster and had a much better rate of climb and diving capability, as well as far superior all-round performance at over 6000 m – although by the time of its service introduction the air war had inexorably turned against the Germans, no matter how capable the D-9 was found to be. Exact production figures for the *Dora-9* are impossible to verify, with a total of approximately 700 probably being a good starting point. Several of the early production *Dora-9* aircraft were involved in test and development work, and a variety of further D-series models were envisaged.

The planned Fw 190D-10, with an engine-mounted MK 108 30 mm cannon, Jumo 213C engine and Ta 152 tail, did not proceed very far, but the Fw 190D-11 was built in small numbers. This model, powered by the Jumo 213F, was armed with two MG 151 20 mm cannons in the wing-roots with 250 rounds per gun (rpg) and two outerwing-mounted 30 mm MK 108 cannons with 85 rpg. Seven 'V' numbered development aircraft (V55 to V61) were converted by Focke-Wulf into D-11 configuration, which amongst other changes (compared to the D-9) included altered engine mounts. The Jumo 213F also had a three-stage supercharger, with a different air intake, rather than the simpler unit of the Jumo 213A. V56 W.Nr. 170924 is believed to have first flown in August 1944. Some 13 D-11 production aircraft are thought to have been built, possibly from recycled Fw 190A-8 airframes at Langenhagen.

The Fw 190D-12 was the first D-series production model to feature a weapon firing through the propeller spinner, this being a single 30 mm MK 108 cannon. A 20 mm MG 151 cannon was mounted in each wing-root. Three *Versuchs* aircraft (converted from A-8 airframes) pioneered the series, which was to be powered by a Jumo 213E or F engine. One of these aircraft reached a very respectable 730 km/h at an altitude of 9150 m.

Production start-up was apparently delayed until at least March 1945 at both Fieseler and Arado due to shortages of the MK 108 weapon, and it is not clear how many production aircraft were subsequently made.

The last production model of the D-series Fw 190 was the Fw 190D-13. This model introduced an MG 151 20 mm cannon firing through the propeller spinner, but was otherwise generally based on the D-12. It had completely flat panelling in front of the windscreen, and as with other late-mark D-series aircraft it was based as closely as possible on the Fw 190A-8 airframe. Two development aircraft were built including the V62, and tested in late 1944 and early 1945. Production commenced at the Arbeits-Gemeinschaft Roland combine as late as March 1945, and approximately 30 aircraft were completed before the end of the war. Most appear to have been fitted with a Jumo 213F-1 engine of some 2060 hp.

As a final twist in the story of the Fw 190, later versions of the D-series were planned with none other than the Daimler-Benz DB 603 inline engine as their powerplant. This proposal suited Focke-Wulf's ideas of powering the Fw 190 with this engine, despite the earlier problems with the Fw 190C programme. A major motivation behind the project was to quickly get a DB 603-engined model into production and service, as the DB 603-engined Ta 152 proposals had been progressing far too slowly. In the event a considerable amount of design work was expended on the DB 603-powered Fw 190D ideas from October 1944 onwards, leading to the D-14 and D-15 models.

These aircraft were eventually overtaken by events at the end of the war, although persistent reports claim that the D-15 was produced in small numbers possibly at Daimler-Benz's Stuttgart facility. This model would have been basically an Fw 190A-8 with a Ta 152C front end and vertical tail.

CHAPTER 8 | TANK'S LONG-SPAN WONDER

THE GERMAN AIRCRAFT industry can be rightly regarded as having created some of the most capable and advanced warplanes of the World War 2 era, and the industry as a whole proved to be highly innovative in developing various new weapons and technologies that were well ahead of their time. It is therefore ironic that many of those who were in charge of the industry on the governmental level in the Third Reich, and indeed some of those at high level within the Luftwaffe itself, had little or no vision or ability to realise the worth of some of this innovation.

The development of a viable high-altitude fighter for the Luftwaffe only became a high priority when Allied bombing missions from high level over the Third Reich began to assume significant proportions – despite the protestations of many in the German aircraft industry that more resources and urgency should have been placed earlier into creating viable high-altitude fighters. Kurt Tank himself came upon this high-level indifference, and on a number of occasions lamented the fact that the Luftwaffe could have had a fighter of the calibre of the Ta 152H earlier in the war if more resources and urgency had been placed on the high-altitude concept.

When it entered production late in 1944, the Ta 152H was representative of the high levels of piston-engine fighter development that had been reached in Germany by the final stages of World War 2. However, the type was never used in the high altitude combat role for which it had been envisaged, and there were far too few examples in service in any case to meaningfully take on the massive numbers of Allied fighters that had by then established air superiority over what was left of the Third Reich. Nevertheless the few Ta 152H models that entered combat at lower levels proved to be dangerous adversaries for the Allied aircraft that they met.

Focke-Wulf intended to have many of these aircraft in production by the end of 1945, and substantial plans had been laid to draw a number of companies into the Ta 152 production programme that had previously not been involved in (or had only been on the periphery of) Fw 190 production.

The story of the Ta 152 really started during 1942, when Focke-Wulf's designers were looking at many ways to increase the Fw 190's performance at higher altitudes. One of the ways to achieve this was the installation of engines that were either of higher power than the BMW 801 radial of the Fw 190A at take-off power, or could deliver more of their useful power at higher altitudes than was possible with the standard BMW engine. Solutions such as these were tried out in the Fw 190B and C-series programmes that did not succeed, as previously described.

The Fw 190D was much more successful, as shown in the previous chapter, but was regarded by Kurt Tank as being largely a stop-gap until something more advanced could be brought into production. Another way of achieving better performance above altitudes of some 6000 m was to radically redesign the Fw 190, or to use its already proven layout as a basis on which to develop improvements for better high-altitude performance. Focke-Wulf's design team came up with a number of possible ideas that combined both of these concepts, and the most important of these were designated between Ra-1 and Ra-6.

Some of these proposals were for comparatively straightforward developments of the Fw 190 layout with different powerplants, but significantly there were also concepts in

The Ta 152C series fighter/fighter-bomber development aircraft W.Nr. 110007 CI+XM (V7) has its engine run in the snow in early 1945. This DB 603-powered aircraft was one of the few specially made Ta 152 development aircraft manufactured at Focke-Wulf's Sorau facility (*Focke-Wulf, Bremen*)

which the Fw 190 was only the basis on which a considerable amount of new design work was arranged. This included the possibility of a completely new, long-span wing of high aspect ratio that would go a long way towards tackling the aerodynamics required for a high-altitude Fw 190 derivative. Focke-Wulf presented a number of these proposals to the RLM's *Technisches Amt* in May 1943.

It was soon recognised that these concepts would form the basis of what was essentially a new aircraft type, and the sum of the Focke-Wulf recommendations received the RLM's numbering 8-152 during August 1943, with Tank's name being brought into the designation to give Ta 152. 8-152 had in fact already been assigned once before, to a Klemm project. The designation Ta 153 also appears to have been given to a Focke-Wulf proposal for a Daimler-Benz engined layout, but this did not proceed far by itself as a separate programme.

As originally conceived, the Ta 152 was to form what was essentially a family of fighter and fighter-bomber versions, with a dedicated reconnaissance model and a two-seat conversion trainer also envisaged. However, work was eventually to progress much more slowly than Tank would have preferred, partly due to official indecision. On the other hand, Messerschmitt had also been invited by the RLM to look at the possibility of creating a viable high-altitude fighter, and some of Messerschmitt's proposals were basically redesigns of the successful Bf 109 layout.

Unfortunately for Focke-Wulf, the following 12 months or so were to see a considerable lack of official decision making and delay. Eventually, the planned Ta 152A and Ta 152B

Known as the Ta 152V7, the Ta 152C series development aircraft CI+XM first flew in January 1945. The Ta 152C was intended as a fighter/fighter-bomber, powered by the DB 603L/LA inline engine, but only a handful of production machines appear to have been made, and even their existence remains contentious (*Focke-Wulf, Bremen*)

The third Ta 152H-0 pre-production aircraft was W.Nr. 150003 CW+CC, and it is seen here almost certainly at Cottbus just after completion. Although superficially resembling the Fw 190D series, the Ta 152H was a very different breed with a considerably altered fuselage, and a totally new long-span wing, amongst other changes (*Focke-Wulf, Bremen*)

medium-altitude fighter and fighter-bomber models did not progress beyond the creation of a number of prototypes, and it was only the high-altitude Ta 152H programme that reached any form of meaningful production status.

The Ta 152H was intended from the start as a dedicated high-altitude fighter. It was to have a pressurised cockpit, lengthened fuselage with redesigned vertical tail surfaces, and a new, long-span wing, amongst many other significant new developments.

The powerplant chosen was the Junkers Jumo 213E, which was intended to be power boosted with GM-1 nitrous oxide as well as MW-50 methanol-water. Exhaust-driven turbo-super-charging, as with all other engines used in production Fw 190 and Ta 152 aircraft, was not available for this powerplant in production form. It was installed in similar fashion to the Jumo 213A-1 in the Fw 190D-9, with an annular radiator in the nose that gave the false impression of a radial-engined arrangement.

Focke-Wulf had planned to embark upon a significant prototype/development aircraft building programme for the whole Ta 152 series, with construction of these new aircraft at Sorau and Adelheide. In the event, however, many of these were cancelled as the general war situation became more pressing, and the need to move on quickly at last started to become very apparent even to those at the highest levels in the German government.

For the Ta 152H programme, a number of already-existing Fw 190s were heavily rebuilt mainly at Adelheide to serve as H-series development aircraft. These included some of the *Versuchs* aircraft that were used in the unsuccessful Fw 190C programme.

Cottbus-built Ta 152H-1 W.Nr. 150167 seen following its capture by US forces at Erfurt-North near the end of the war in Europe. The considerably different fuselage proportions of the Ta 152 compared to the Fw 190A series aircraft are evident in this view (*John Batchelor Archive*)

The first true Ta 152H-standard aircraft to fly (it was pre-dated by several development aircraft for the Ta 152A and B-series) was the Fw 190V33/U1 W.Nr. 0058 GH+KW (an original Fw 190A-0 or A-1 machine) which first flew in Ta 152H configuration on 13 July 1944. The second true H-series *Versuchs* aircraft, Fw 190V30/U1 W.Nr. 0055 GH+KT, flew on 6 August. Unfortunately both of these aircraft were lost in crashes after only a short time, thus putting back an already delayed programme. Eventually, a number of other development aircraft joined the H-series effort, including the much modified and rebuilt Fw 190V18 W.Nr. 0040 CF+OY that had previously featured prominently in the ultimately unsuccessful Fw 190C programme.

Manufacture of the Ta 152H-0 pre-production aircraft commenced at Cottbus in November 1944. This was well before proper testing had been completed for the H-series, and test pilot Hans Sander later stated that some of the airframe stress analysis for the Ta 152H (work that is normally carried out on the ground with a static test airframe) was actually performed in the air due to the shortage of time available, and the growing difficulty of performing this work on the ground. A general intention was to base the Ta 152 airframe as closely as possible

on the Fw 190A-8 to facilitate construction using the same jigs where possible. However, the Ta 152H was a very different aircraft to the Fw 190A-8.

The fuselage, although resembling the Fw 190's layout, was altered in a number of ways. The installation of the Jumo 213E inline engine was accomplished in similar fashion to that in the late Fw 190D models that used this engine, with a lengthened nose and rear fuselage, but there was additional length built-in in several places, and repositioning to give an overall length of 10.710 m. The vertical tail was considerably widened to give additional directional stability – this widened type tail was also incorporated in some of the very late model BMW 801-powered Fw 190 production aircraft as mentioned previously.

Although its structure was metal to begin with, there is evidence that some later production Ta 152Hs actually had wooden tail structures due again to the worsening war situation. The Ta 152H's cockpit was pressurised, the earlier problems with breaking cockpit covers encountered in the Fw 190C series having been largely overcome. However, full testing of the Ta 152's pressurisation layout was never fully carried out, and the operational Ta 152Hs that flew in combat did so largely at comparatively low level.

A detail view of the port side rear fuselage of a Ta 152. The open hatch served as access for various systems and equipment. In earlier models of the Fw 190, this hatch was specifically for access to the aircraft's radio compartment, and it was possible for a human to climb inside. Groundcrew members or other interested and intrepid parties would sometimes be transported within the fuselage of Fw 190s during unit redeployments (*Focke-Wulf, Bremen*)

The most radical change was in the Ta 152H's wing structure, which was unlike anything seen on any of the Fw 190 production models. Gone was the standard wing of 10.50 m of all the preceding Fw 190 series production models, to be replaced with a long-span fuel-carrying wing of 14.44 m. In fact the wing fitted to the Ta 152H-0 pre-production aircraft was somewhat different to the wing as fitted to the H-1 series.

The H-0 aircraft did not have the GM-1 nitrous oxide and MW-50 methanol-water boost systems fitted, and featured a simpler wing internal layout. The H-1 production series was intended to be fitted with a different wing structure, with each wing carrying three internal fuel tanks – the inner port wing tank was for the MW-50 system. A tank for the GM-1 boost system's nitrous oxide was installed behind the cockpit in the H-1.

The wing was fitted in a different position compared to the Fw 190 relative to the cockpit, which itself had been slightly relocated due to the rearrangement of the fuselage in the lengthened Ta 152 layout. A further change comprised the substitution of the Fw 190's very effective electric undercarriage retraction system with a hydraulic system for the Ta 152.

With the Jumo 213E engine fitted – production H-1 models were intended for the Jumo 213E-1 development – the Ta 152H enjoyed excellent performance capabilities. As previously related, the Fw 190V29/U1 was able to reach 13,654 m on one epic flight, and the Ta 152H's maximum speed was 718 km/h at 10,700 m. These figures were unheard of even for the Fw 190D series, and the Ta 152H also appeared to be more manoeuvrable than the *Dora-9* as well – although comparisons are difficult to draw due to the comparative lack of testing and operational experience of the Ta 152H.

Standard armament for the Ta 152H-1 was one 30 mm MK 108 firing through the propeller spinner and two 20 mm MG 151 cannons, one in each wing root.

Production of the 43 Ta 152Hs known to have been built was carried out at Focke-Wulf's Cottbus facility, this total comprising 20 H-0 pre-production models and 23 H-1 production examples. There is also some documentary evidence to suggest that a solitary Ta 152H-2 was also built. The H-series was the only Ta 152 model that was manufactured in any quantity, but two other models, the Ta 152C and the Ta 152E, also appear to have been built in small numbers.

The Ta 152C was a planned fighter-bomber model, powered by the Daimler-Benz DB 603LA engine and featuring a shorter-span wing of 11 m. Delays with the powerplant and the late start of this programme conspired with other problems to ensure that only a handful were built. Production appears to have been carried out very late in the war by ATG in Leipzig and by Siebel at a factory at Schkeuditz, between Leipzig and Halle. The Ta 152E was a dedicated reconnaissance model of which at least two were apparently made at Erfurt-North by Mimetall, although this programme remains something of a mystery.

CHAPTER 9

ARMAMENT

FOCKE-WULF'S DESIGNERS intended the Fw 190 to be a well-armed aeroplane, and devised a structure that was strong enough to carry a useful internal selection of guns and/or cannons, together with a practical external load, while including growth potential as the design developed. This was an important contrast to the Bf 109, which although able to carry a useful selection of weapons, was nevertheless left behind by the formidable weapons line-up available to the Fw 190 as operational experience, modifications and design changes added to the latter type's versatility and range of firepower.

There were basically three internal weapons stations designed in the BMW 801-powered Fw 190 models, although the third was not always used. The first weapons station was the upper forward fuselage location, ahead of the windscreen. In early production A-series Fw 190s, this was the position for the

An early Fw 190 has its guns test-fired and synchronised at the firing butts at Bremen (*Focke-Wulf, Bremen*)

This detail view shows the installation of two MG 131 13 mm machine guns in the upper forward fuselage weapons station of a late model Fw 190. This installation was introduced into production versions in the Fw 190A-7 series, and it replaced the previous rather inadequate armament of two MG 17 machine guns of 7.9 mm calibre (*Focke-Wulf, Bremen*)

two MG 17 7.9 mm machine guns, often disparagingly known as 'door knockers'. From the Fw 190A-7 onwards they were replaced by two harder-hitting MG 131 13 mm machine guns. These weapons were installed in StL 131/5B fixed mountings, and were fed by two fuselage ammunition boxes (one for each gun), each containing up to 475 rounds.

Despite the alterations made to the forward fuselage of the basic Fw 190 design to accommodate the Jumo 213 engine in the Fw 190D-9 model, this weapons station was retained in that version, and was able to accommodate the two MG 131 machine guns as carried by the Fw 190A series and related aircraft.

The second weapons station was in the wing-roots. In the later versions of the Fw 190A series, and similar ground attack or fighter-bomber models, this was the location for an MG 151 20 mm cannon in each wing-root, mounted on an StL 151/2B fixed mount. Each cannon's barrel was housed in a blast tube, and ammunition was held in two ammunition boxes (one for

The neat installation of the two Rheinmetall-Borsig MG 17 7.9 mm machine guns in the upper forward fuselage weapons station of all production A-model Fw 190s up to and including the Fw 190A-6 (*Focke-Wulf, Bremen*)

A close-up view of the installation of two MG 17 7.9 mm machine guns in the upper forward fuselage of Fw 190V5 W.Nr. 0005 – the first aircraft to carry armament in this fuselage location (*Focke-Wulf, Bremen*)

A detail view of the breeches of the two MG 17 7.9 mm machine guns fitted in early and mid-production Fw 190A aircraft (*Focke-Wulf, Bremen*)

Looking up into the Fw 190's inner main undercarriage bays, it was possible to see the barrel of the wing-root mounted armament. In this case the weapon appears to be the MG 17 7.9 mm machine-gun as fitted in the Fw 190A-1 in that location (*Focke-Wulf, Bremen*)

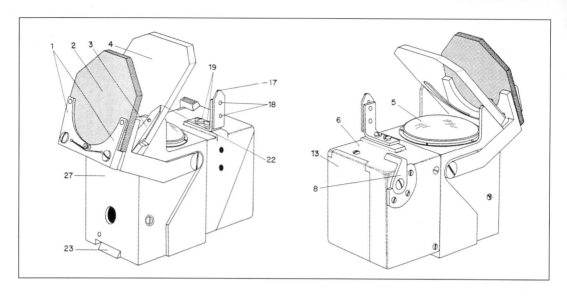

each gun), fitted within the fuselage behind the main spar. Each ammunition box held 250 rounds.

The third weapons station was in the outer wing area, just outboard of the main undercarriage attachments. In early Fw 190A series aircraft this was the home of the rather unsatisfactory MG FF 20 mm cannon, and in service this weapon was often removed altogether – either because it was generally unsatisfactory, or to save weight in the fighter-bomber or ground attack versions. From the Fw 190A-6 onwards, the far more satisfactory MG 151 20 mm cannon was fitted on an StL 151/11 fixed mount. Each gun was mounted on its side to facilitate the ammunition feed, but the actual positioning of the weapon in the wing was also lowered compared to the original MG FF attachments. An ammunition box with up to 140 rounds was provided for each gun, mounted outboard of the weapon.

With their barrels housed in blast tubes, these cannons were not synchronised because they lay outside the propeller arc, unlike the guns in the other weapons stations. In some models, notably the *Sturm* anti-bomber Fw 190s, the outboard

Front and rear three-quarter drawings of the Revi 16B gunsight as fitted to Fw 190A-7 and later models of the Fw 190, replacing the earlier Revi C12D. It was fitted offset slightly to the right in the Fw 190's cockpit. Important features are the main focusing lens (5) and lens chamber (27), as well as the reflector plate (4) on which the illuminated sighting image was projected when the internal light bulb (inside housing 13) was switched on. The sight could also be used as a simple mechanical 'manual' sight using the rear sighting post (17) and forward post-type projection (22) (*Focke-Wulf, Bremen*)

Two Rheinmetall-Borsig MG 131 13 mm machine guns were fitted in the upper forward fuselage weapons station from the Fw 190A-7 onwards, replacing the MG 17 machine gun in that location. Here, two MG 131 cannons are shown on a test installation in the Focke-Wulf Bremen factory (*Focke-Wulf, Bremen*)

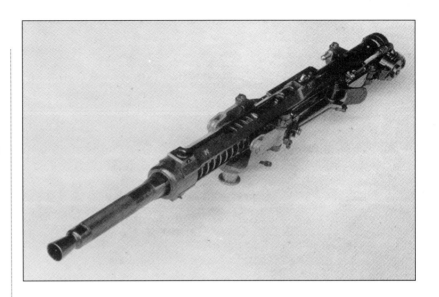

The Oerlikon MG FF 20 mm cannon, as shown here, was fitted in the outer weapons station in the mid-wing area of the Fw 190A just outboard of the main undercarriage legs. It was replaced in that location from the Fw 190A-6 onwards by the much more satisfactory Mauser MG 151 20 mm cannon (*Focke-Wulf, Bremen*)

weapons station instead housed a formidable MK 108 30 mm cannon in each wing.

The two principal manufacturers of the Fw 190's guns were Mauser and Rheinmetall-Borsig. The former company was responsible for the MG 151, whose designation relevant to the weapon fitted in the Fw 190 was MG 151/20 or /20E. Development of this weapon had started from the mid-1930s onwards, and it matured into a thoroughly dependable and hard-hitting cannon that was a major reason for the success of many pilots flying the Fw 190. It weighed 42.5 kg and had a rate of fire of 780 to 800 rounds per minute for the unsynchronised and 550 to 750 rounds per minute for the synchronised versions. In the Fw 190, it entirely replaced the Oerlikon (Bekker) MG FF 20 mm cannon.

Rheinmettal-Borsig was responsible for the MG 17 and MG 131 machine guns, and the MK 108 30 mm cannon as used in the Fw 190. The latter weapon was probably the hardest-hitting of any of the cannons regularly used by German fighters during the war, and it was by far the most effective cannon employed against US bomber formations in the later stages of the war.

As previously described, a number of external weapons carriers were employed for the attack models of the Fw 190. These included the ubiquitous ETC 501 stores mounting beneath the fuselage, and a number of possible stores attachments beneath the wings outboard of the undercarriage. The Fw 190 could carry the standard general-purpose bombs used by the Luftwaffe, including the SC 50 (50-kg), SC 250 (250-kg) and SC 500 (500-kg), plus other free-fall munitions.

Normally, a bomb of up to 500 kg could be hung under the fuselage, although with some modification a bomb of 1000 kg could also be carried there. The theoretical maximum external load was some 1000 kg. This could include a 500-kg bomb beneath the fuselage plus (on later examples) a 250-kg bomb beneath each wing on an ETC 503 pylon, although more usually for battlefield support ground attack, the load would be

A close-up of the attachment points for the ETC 501 stores rack, as well as the stabilising bars for the underfuselage 300-litre external fuel tank. The latter was cleared for use by all Fw 190 models (*Focke-Wulf, Bremen*)

Attack and fighter-bomber versions of the Fw 190 usually carried bombs of no more than 500-kg beneath the fuselage, suspended from an ETC 501 stores rack. However, trials were carried out with much larger weapons such as the 1000-kg bomb shown here, which needed the removal of its lower fin to allow sufficient ground clearance. The trials/development aircraft is probably Fw 190A-5 W.Nr. 151286 (*Focke-Wulf, Bremen*)

a 500- or 250-kg bomb beneath the fuselage (or four 50-kg bombs on an ER 4 adapter rack), plus two 50-kg bombs beneath each wing on ETC 50 racks. However, there were various possible weapons combinations. Later in the war a variety of air-to-ground rockets were carried under the wings of attack models of the Fw 190, including the *Panzerschreck* and *Panzerblitz* weapons.

A wide variety of other weapons were carried operationally by Fw 190 models. This included various *Rüstsatz* field conversion kits, numbering amongst these being underwing gun/cannon-equipped pods or fairings. As stated elsewhere, an important underwing store used against formations of heavy bombers was the 21-cm WGr 21 mortar rocket, which was usually associated with the designation /R6. This weapon was

On-going trials with early Fw 190 aircraft included the evaluation of various possible weapons installations. The trial ground attack layout shown here included two 50-kg bombs beneath each wing on simplified carriers, and four 50-kg bombs beside each other beneath the fuselage. This particular layout was not adopted for production aircraft (*Focke-Wulf, Bremen*)

An Fw 190A-4/R6, possibly W.Nr. 781 (therefore probably Focke-Wulf-built 140781), carries a single launch tube beneath each wing for the WGr 21 21 cm mortar rocket system. A completely unguided air-to-air weapon, the WGr could only be used with any effect against large formations of daylight bombers, although in this role it duly proved devastating in breaking up enemy formations (*Focke-Wulf, Bremen*)

One of the many attempts to up-gun the offensive capability of the Fw 190 was the installation of a WB 151-type gondola beneath each wing, each pod containing two MG 151 20 mm cannons. Two trials/development Fw 190s were converted in what came to be designated the Fw 190A-5/U12 configuration. One of these, Focke-Wulf-built W.Nr. 150813 BH+CC, is shown here. The configuration was later used as the Fw 190A-8/R1 *(Focke-Wulf, Bremen)*

also used less regularly against ground targets. Some specific *Rüstsatz* conversions were the preserve of particular companies.

For example, the /R1 used by the Fw 190A-6/R1 fighter (and possibly the G-3/R1) comprised lower wing-mounted WB 151 gun-pods of two 20 mm MG 151 cannons. This work was subcontracted to the LZA works at Küpper near Sagan (which is yet another former German location associated with the Fw 190 that is now in present-day Poland), this company being an Arado subsidiary organisation. Some 60 Fw 190s were fitted with these gun pods by the end of November 1943.

Various air-to-air weapons concepts were also experimented with using trials Fw 190s, including the upwards-firing fuselage-mounted SG 116 *Zellendusche* battery of three MK 103 30 mm cannons. In this case, the weapons would have been triggered by a photo-electric cell, when the carrying aircraft flew beneath a bomber formation. A similar principle was proposed for the so-called *Rohrblock* upwards-firing battery of seven 30 mm MK 108 cannon barrels.

An enormous variety of weapons proposals were experimented with by various Fw 190s that were delegated for test purposes. Some of these weapons were extremely exotic, such as

The potential firepower of the Fw 190 was increased in this trial installation of a gun pod beneath each wing replacing the MG FF cannons within the wing outboard of the main undercarriage. Each pod contained a long-barrel MK 103 30 mm cannon. The development aircraft shown here is Fw 190A-5/U11 W.Nr. 151303, built by Focke-Wulf *(Focke-Wulf, Bremen)*

the downwards-firing anti-tank cannons mounted almost vertically in, and through, the wings of at least one trials Fw 190F. In this case the weapon, designated SG 113A, was supposed to be triggered at low level by the target tank's magnetic field. Needless to say this weapon did not see operational service, although some success was claimed in trials against real tanks that were of course not fighting back.

Weapons such as the *Gero* flame-thrower were also envisaged for Fw 190 use. The Blohm und Voss Bv 246 *Hagelkorn* (Hailstone) glider bomb was actually flown and launched in various trials from beneath the fuselage of several test Fw 190s, but never used operationally. A 'bouncing-bomb' type weapon, the *Kurt* SB 800RC rolling mine-bomb, was also test flown and launched by at least one trials Fw 190 but, again, never used in combat. Focke-Wulf's designers had a particular love affair with the idea of employing the Fw 190 as a torpedo-carrier, and almost every version of the Fw 190 was either designated for or examples were actually test-flown with a number of torpedo or torpedo-bomb type weapons. Even a torpedo-carrying model of the Ta 152 was envisaged. Again, little or indeed no operational use resulted from all that expenditure of design resources.

Much more practical were experiments with advanced air-to-air weapons. The Fw 190 was used in important trials for the Ruhrstahl X-4 wire-guided air-to-air missile, which was undergoing significant development in the final stages of the war. The X-4 was two metres long and powered by a BMW 109-548 liquid-fuel rocket motor of some 140 kg thrust. Several Fw 190s of different types were involved in flight testing and test launching these advanced weapons, which were primarily intended for use by the Messerschmitt Me 262 jet fighter. Also associated with the Fw 190 was the R4M *Orkan* (Hurricane) air-to-air rocket, which was used by some Fw 190D-9 in combat, but found wider operational use by the Me 262 in the closing months of the war. This weapon would also have been used by the Ta 152 if there had been time following that type's combat début.

Focke-Wulf's designers had a strange love affair with the idea of using the Fw 190 as a torpedo carrier, and virtually all marks of the Fw 190 were involved in plans for torpedo-carrying models. Some of these reached the test stage, but in reality the Fw 190 was rarely if ever used operationally in torpedo strikes against Allied shipping. Illustrated is the Fw 190A-5/U14, probably W.Nr. 150871 TD+SI, carrying an LTF 5B torpedo on a special ETC 502 underfuselage stores rack (*MAP*)

CHAPTER 10

OVERVIEW OF Fw 190 PRODUCTION

PRODUCTION OF THE Fw 190 took place at a significant number of major sites and smaller locations, and the supply of relevant components to these centres came from an even greater number of large and small companies. A variety of concerns were additionally involved in recycling and rebuilding old Fw 190s into newer models, or in simply repairing badly damaged examples. That much we do know as a basis of a study of the production of the Fw 190, and in the Appendices of this book the major players in the production process are listed.

It is interesting to note that the Luftwaffe took on charge 224 Fw 190s in the first year of production (1941), and that this figure rose to 1878 in 1942. In 1943 it climbed to 3208 and in 1944 it had risen to approximately 11,411. In 1945, up to the German capitulation, the figure stood at some 2700. By these later years, however, the production infrastructure for all aircraft types and component suppliers within Germany had been severely disrupted by Allied bombing, so that aircraft taken on strength were not necessarily combat-ready, properly kitted-out with the correct equipment, or built to the highest standards. Increasingly as the war progressed, less skilled workers were drawn into the production process by a number of companies, and several organisations 'employed' foreign workers whose willingness to toil to the highest standards in the cause of the Third Reich was understandably open to question.

Attentive readers will have noted that several names in particular have appeared with regularity in the descriptions elsewhere in this book of the production of the diverse Fw 190 models. In particular, Arado, Fieseler and AGO were highly significant in the building of the Fw 190 aside from the parent company.

Arado of Warnemünde began life as the Arado Handelsgesellschaft mbH in 1925, and became the Arado Flugzeugwerke GmbH in 1933, although the history of aircraft manufacture in that area stretched back to the World War 1 era.

Situated on the northern coast of Germany near the historic Hanseatic port of Rostock, Warnemünde eventually became one of the principal aircraft manufacturing sites in the Third Reich.

This situation came about through considerable state interference, as Arado's senior partner, Heinrich Lübbe, and other important Arado personnel resisted Nazi attempts from 1933 onwards to integrate the company into making aeroplanes for the re-created Luftwaffe. Lübbe was arrested in 1935 and stripped of his position, the German government successfully taking over total control of the company.

From 1941 Arado was increasingly integrated into the licence manufacturing programme for the Fw 190, and eventually at least 3944 Fw 190s were built by the company principally at Warnemünde and Tutow, with assemblies supplied by the Arado Anklam plant. The decentralised Arado facilities at Malchin and Greifswald were also involved with Fw 190 parts assembly, and the major company site at Brandenburg/Neuendorf also contributed to the overall effort. Warnemünde, like Focke-Wulf's base at Bremen, was a comparatively easy target to locate, and it received its first major air raid from the RAF on the night of 8/9 May 1942. Increasingly, Fw 190 production sites such as this were targeted by both the RAF and the USAAF, as the Allies sought to strike at German fighters in the places where they were being manufactured.

Few published sources on the Fw 190 include a photograph of Erhard Milch, yet it was Milch who was highly important in the planning and execution of production direction that led to so many Focke-Wulf fighters being produced. Milch was involved to one extent or another with aircraft production for a large part of the existence of the Third Reich, and his significance considerably grew following the suicide of Ernst Udet in 1941. It all ended in 1944 following arguments over production of the Me 262, with Albert Speer's armaments ministry subsequently taking over much of the production direction. Milch was convicted and imprisoned after the war for the use and transportation of foreign workers in the German aircraft industry, and died in comparative obscurity in 1972 (John Batchelor Archive)

Production sites for the Fw 190 became important targets for the Allied bombing campaign. This bombing was at times highly effective, and the most spectacular raid of them all took place on 9 October 1943. That day, Eighth Air Force 'heavies' caused considerable destruction at Focke-Wulf's Marienburg facility, with the bombers placing 83 per cent of their bombs within 610 m of the aiming point – one of the finest examples of daylight precision bombing during the whole war. In this view, B-17F Flying Fortresses of the 94th Bomb Group (letter 'A' in a white square marking), having bombed apparently unopposed, leave a large plume of smoke emitting from the Marienburg factory (*USAAF*)

The Fieseler company owed its existence to the celebrated aerobatic pilot Gerhard Fieseler, and was created out of the Segel Flugzeugbau Kassel, which he purchased in 1930. Always based in the Kassel area, Fieseler's main plant from the start was at Kassel-Bettenhausen. The company became the Gerhard Fieseler Werke GmbH in the first half of 1939. In the early war years a new plant was established at Kassel-Waldau, and this was involved very soon in Fw 190 manufacture. Later, the Bettenhausen facilities were also brought into the programme. Fieseler's production of Fw 190s ran to at least 2155 examples, and was probably somewhat more than this.

One of the most important employers in the Oschersleben area, the AGO company was formed in 1934, an original AGO concern having existed at Berlin-Johannisthal before World War 1. AGO (sometimes simply written in lower case as 'Ago') was established to undertake licensed manufacture of aircraft, under the name AGO Flugzeugwerke GmbH. The company became one of the principal licence suppliers of the Fw 190 from the A-2 version onwards, with production reaching an early peak of approximately 50 new aircraft a month in 1942.

Like most other Fw 190 producers, AGO was a significant target for Allied bombing, receiving its first major visit by the Eighth Force on 28 July 1943 (Fieseler's Kassel facilities were also a target for that raid). Although this first attack was not serious for AGO, others in early 1944 (including a significant raid on 11 January) resulted in large damage, and in consequence a considerable relocation of the company's production organisation in the Oschersleben and surrounding areas.

An overall result of the Allied bombing was the commencement of the use, by some sectors of the German aircraft industry, of underground or semi-underground, reinforced and widely dispersed facilities. This created a considerable dislocation of normal production methods and procedures, as well as creating further delays as these facilities were built. Under the *Waldwerk* scheme, assembly facilities of some companies were dispersed to camouflaged, out of the way forest locations, while underground facilities known generically as *Bunkerwerke* were intended for several specific aircraft-producing programmes. The hard work of building these sites was often performed by slave labour from concentration camps or similar facilities.

At least two underground or semi-underground plants were proposed for Fw 190 production, including the REIMAHG factory south of Jena, although this was switched to Me 262 work before any Fw 190s were built there. US forces entering Germany at the end of the war discovered an underground factory at Gevelsberg that had been repairing, or possibly recycling, Fw 190 versions into later marks.

Major repair facilities for Luftwaffe aircraft were located all over the Third Reich and occupied countries, and included many companies that one would not normally associate with the Fw 190. The German national airline, Deutsche Lufthansa, like its modern-day counterpart, possessed a number of highly professional technical and repair facilities in several locations. Some of these were involved in repair work on Luftwaffe aircraft, including Fw 190s. Amongst them were facilities in Berlin, at Travemünde, and at Praha-Ruzyn airport in the Protectorate of Bohemia and Moravia (the modern-day Czech Republic – a number of Fw 190-operating units were based in the Czech lands during the war, and Praha-Ruzyn was also a training base for Fw 190-equipped *Mistel* composite aircraft). Interestingly, Lufthansa was intended as a producer of two-seat Ta 152 trainers had World War 2 continued for longer than it did.

This photograph of an unidentified maintenance or recycling facility shows one of the reasons why it is so difficult to pinpoint the exact number of Fw 190s that were built. Major work is being carried out on a number of diverse Fw 190s. Facilities such as this existed in a variety of locations in Germany and in occupied countries, and precise documentation from these centres will probably never come to light
(*John Batchelor Archive*)

CHAPTER 11

FRONTLINE

An early Fw 190A – probably an A-2 of II./JG 26 – is quietly worked on at a French or Belgian airfield. JG 26 was the first Luftwaffe fighter wing to operate the Fw 190. As with so many contemporary photographs, the German censor has been at work, with the cockpit canopy having been painted out (*via Chris Ellis*)

THE FIGHTING MACHINE that Focke-Wulf's designers had created for the Luftwaffe in the form of the Fw 190 turned out to be one of the most formidable and capable aircraft to serve in World War 2. The first Fw 190s to enter service were the A-1 aircraft of II.*Gruppe* of JG 26, which received its first aircraft in late July/early August 1941, and began using them operationally in combat over northern France, Belgium and the English Channel just weeks later. They gradually achieved considerable success against RAF fighters, including the Spitfire V, to the point where the British found it difficult to counter the Fw 190 in the spring and early summer of 1942 as growing numbers of the Focke-Wulf fighters entered frontline operation.

Indeed, it was only with the gradual RAF service entry of the Spitfire IX, with its Merlin 61 engine featuring a two-stage

supercharger, that the situation began to improve. Nevertheless, for the rest of the war the Fw 190 remained a very respectable opponent. This was particularly true when it was flown by experienced pilots, although the availability of these became less and less as the war went on.

The BMW 801-powered Fw 190's comparative lack of performance at higher altitudes was to become an important shortcoming, particularly when the fighter was expected to take on the ever-growing numbers of USAAF B-17 Flying Fortress and B-24 Liberator bombers high in the skies over Germany and occupied Europe. Although successful in the bomber interceptor role, it became an increasingly different case when the Fw 190s had to take on American escort fighters as well.

From the early months of 1944, the Merlin-engined P-51 Mustang in particular became increasingly widespread, with its capability to escort the bombers all the way to their targets deep in Germany and back to their bases in England. This was a high-altitude war against increasingly prevalent and very dangerous, well-equipped opponents. The high-level shortcomings in terms of comparative engine performance were addressed with the Junkers Jumo 213-engined Fw 190D-9, which entered operational service with III.*Gruppe* of JG 54 in October 1944. This aircraft was a formidable fighter in its own right, but by that time the crucial battle for air superiority in the skies over its homeland had been lost.

The high ground was also the preserve of the Ta 152, although it came far too late to affect the course of the war for the Germans. The first Ta 152s were delivered to III.*Gruppe* of

Lined up on the grass, a clutch of Fw 190A-2s or A-3 sit awaiting their next mission. The Fw 190 had few problems operating from grass, and its wide-track main undercarriage prevented it from having the ground-looping problems that were encountered by the Bf 109 with its narrow main undercarriage. These Fw 190s are from JG 2 or possibly JG 1, operating over the English Channel in 1942. Note the Bf 109s parked in the background
(*via John Batchelor Archive*)

JG 301 in late January 1945, and the type became operational in March of that year.

At lower levels the Fw 190 was undoubtedly a great success. This was additionally reflected in the significance of the type in low-level air-to-ground missions, where it grew into being one of the best ground attack aircraft and longer-range fighter-bombers of the war. Indeed, the Fw 190 ended up flying with the Luftwaffe on all the war fronts that the German war machine fought on, where it made an impressive contribution to the Axis war effort.

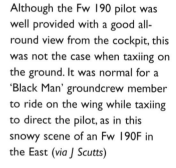

Although the Fw 190 pilot was well provided with a good all-round view from the cockpit, this was not the case when taxiing on the ground. It was normal for a 'Black Man' groundcrew member to ride on the wing while taxiing to direct the pilot, as in this snowy scene of an Fw 190F in the East (*via J Scutts*)

Eastern Front warriors. Lined-up and very colourful, these Fw 190F ground attack aircraft belong to II./SG 1 (Schl.G 1) at Deblin-Irena in Poland. At the time this photograph was taken – probably early 1943 – the unit was transitioning onto the Fw 190F from the Bf 109, and was later to see significant service against Soviet forces (*via R L Ward*)

A late-model Fw 190F of SG 2 on the Eastern Front. When operating from snow-covered or other poor surfaces, the lower part of the Fw 190's main undercarriage doors would often be removed. F-models were a significant component of the German armed forces fighting in the East (*via R L Ward*)

A multitude of pilots scored significant numbers of air-to-air victories in the Fw 190, and the type became the preferred mount of many of the Luftwaffe's top *Experten* (aces). Such well-known pilots as Walter Nowotny, Heinz Bär, Josef Priller, Hannes Trautloft and Walter Oesau, to name but a few, were amongst the many who flew the Fw 190 successfully in combat. Even some of the pilots of the low-level attack Fw 190s were able to claim impressive numbers of aerial victories. The top-scoring attack Fw 190 pilot was Oberleutnant August Lambert of SG 2 and SG 77, who scored 116 aerial victories in the east

A long-standing and successful operator of the Fw 190 was JG 1, which was one of several principal fighter wings that operated Fw 190 fighter versions during the war. In a very wintry scene probably taken during 1943, JG 1 aircraft with distinctive black and white striped cowls line up for take-off (*via R L Ward*)

ABOVE One of the great personalities amongst the Luftwaffe's *Experten* (aces) who flew the Fw 190 was Josef 'Pips' Priller, who rose to become *geschwaderkommodore* of JG 26. Most famous for being one of the few Luftwaffe pilots to see combat over the Allied beachheads on D-Day, 6 June 1944, Priller flew a succession of Fw 190A models marked with his ace-of-hearts personal marking – and also drove a BMW open-top tourer, into which he is being helped in this view by an obergefreiter ground personnel (*John Batchelor Archive*)

BELOW Illustrative of the harsh conditions in which man and machine operated on the Eastern Front, an Fw 190F, possibly of SG 2, is readied for a mission, guided out by several 'Black Men', including one steering at the tail wheel. Note the empty ETC 50-type wing bomb racks outboard of the main undercarriage, and a lack of lower main undercarriage doors. Production of the Fw 190G series fighter-bomber was superseded by continued production of the F-series during 1944 (*via Chris Ellis*)

before being shot down and killed by US fighters in April 1945. Almost certainly the pilot with the most aerial victories in the Fw 190 was Oberleutnant Otto Kittel of JG 54, who claimed most of his 267 aerial victories in the east in the Focke-Wulf fighter. He was shot down and killed during February 1945 in combat with Soviet Ilyushin Il-2s over the Courland pocket.

Despite its very short time in combat, the Ta 152H also proved to be a capable fighter in which several pilots scored aerial victories. Of these, Oberfeldwebel Josef Keil of JG 301 is believed to have been the only pilot to achieve five victories, thus becoming the Ta 152's sole ace.

HIT AND RUN

Although the Fw 190 models intended as and specifically configured for fighter-bomber operations are comparatively well known, some of their individual missions are less well documented. Initially, some of the Luftwaffe's fighter-bomber Fw 190s were organised into specialised *Jabostaffeln* within established fighter wings. In the West, Fw 190 *Jabo* operations came to include low-level missions across the English Channel, with attacks carried out against targets in southern England and London. They involved low-level dashes across the Channel to avoid, as far as possible, radar detection, and to negate the chance of interception by standing patrols of defending fighters, the raiders would retire quickly back across the Channel following the attack itself. Such hit and run missions were

A line-up of various Fw 190 models, with an Fw 190A-4/U8 (Fw 190G-1) *Jabo-Rei* nearest. Some of SKG 10's Fw 190s that were involved in the Bournemouth raid of 23 May 1943 are believed to have been of this type, carrying a 250- or 500-kg bomb beneath the fuselage and a 300-litre external fuel tank under each wing (*Focke-Wulf, Bremen*)

usually escorted by defending fighters sometimes from the fighter wing to which the *Jabos* were attached.

Some of these raids have become well known, such as the attack on Canterbury in Kent during late October 1942 which was a retaliatory mission in response to Allied bombing of German cities. This raid involved the *Jabo* elements of JG 2 and JG 26, together with pilots from ZG 2. However, from late 1942 onwards there was a profound change in the administrative organisation of the Fw 190 *Jabo* units in the West, with the creation within *Luftflotte* 3 of a specialised fast fighter-bomber wing to operate these aircraft.

Schnellkampfgeschwader 10 (SKG 10) was brought into existence from December 1942 (the headquarters *Stab.*/SKG 10 was formed during that month), and this new wing eventually took over the *Jabo* assets of JG 2 (10(*Jabo*)./JG 2) and of JG 26, which came to SKG 10 via JG 54. In addition a number of brand new *Jabostaffeln* were created specifically for the new SKG 10. This *Geschwader* was soon equipped with a mixed bag of Fw 190s that included Fw 190A-4/U8 and Fw 190A-5/U8 *Jabos*, and it embarked on a variety of missions over southern England, including some nocturnal attacks on London.

Famously, several of the unit's Focke-Wulfs landed in error at Kentish airfields during night raids in the spring and summer of 1943. Contrary to some published sources, however, SKG 10's operations in north-west Europe and elsewhere were not flown exclusively at night. SKG 10 also operated in the Mediterranean.

Illustrative of the type of mission performed by SKG 10 against southern England is the devastating raid carried out in broad daylight on Sunday 23 May 1943 against the south coast town of Bournemouth (Hastings, in Kent, was also attacked that same day). At that time in Hampshire, but now in the county of Dorset, Bournemouth is a seaside town with little strategic military importance. However, the nearby town of Christchurch was at that time the site of an important aircraft manufacturing facility (Airspeed at Somerford), and to the west, the port of Poole was later to play a major role during the D-Day operations in June 1944. These do not seem to have been the intended targets for the 23 May raid, however.

It has instead been suggested by some historians that Bournemouth was a target because the town had become a reception centre for Royal Canadian Air Force (RCAF) personnel on arrival in Britain, prior to their being posted to operational or further training units. It has also been proposed that the attack was carried out as a reprisal for the famous 'Dams Raid' by the RAF's No 617 Sqn, which had taken place several days previously. Whatever the motivation, elements of SKG 10 including aircraft from II. and IV./SKG 10 took off from northern France (II./SKG 10 was headquartered at Caen-Carpiquet airfield) at around 1230 hrs on 23 May, and headed with their fighter escort across the English Channel. They were led by Austrian-born Leutnant Leopold 'Poldi' Wenger.

The attacking force made landfall east of Boscombe Pier near a prominent local natural landmark named Hengistbury Head just approaching 1300 hrs. A mixed selection of some 22 Fw 190A-4/U8 and A-5/U8 *Jabos* appears to have made up the strike force – on 17 May 1943 SKG 10 reported a strength of no fewer than 109 available A-4 and A-5 aircraft. The attacking force then wheeled inland to the west from its landfall and swept over the Boscombe area at 1302 hrs, with some elements flying right across the centre of Bournemouth itself.

Bombs rained down in an apparently haphazard fashion, with several of the aircraft also taking the opportunity to shoot up any apparently suitable targets that presented themselves. With the local flak defences rapidly going into action, a considerable amount of small and medium anti-aircraft fire was quickly put up.

Two Fw 190s were shot down (five were actually claimed by the town's defences), one of the attackers (from 15./SKG 10) crashing into Grove Road east of Bournemouth town centre, apparently starting a fire in the St Ives Hotel. The second was seen to go into the sea off Bournemouth Pier. The local newspaper, the *Bournemouth Daily Echo*, claimed the day after the raid that the Grove Road Fw 190 had been shot down by an RAF fighter. Its pilot, Unteroffizier Karl Schmidt, was killed.

The Bournemouth Pier Fw 190 has been attributed to anti-aircraft gunners from the Royal Artillery stationed on the roof of Beales department store in the town centre. One of the gunners involved, Lance Bombardier Norman Lawrence of the 87th Light Anti-Aircraft Regiment, was later awarded the British Empire Medal for his actions that day.

Their mission accomplished, the remaining Fw 190s at once headed for the comparative safety of the English Channel, and a fast dash for their bases. Years later, a piece of the Grove Road Focke-Wulf came to light, having been kept by one of the work party that cleared the crash site in the following days. A section of the main undercarriage retraction mechanism, it was put on display at the Bournemouth Aviation Museum in 2002.

Across the Bournemouth area, the raid had left a trail of destruction. In the town centre, Beales department store had been completely wrecked and was on fire. Several other prominent local buildings had also been hit, in addition to residential property. The official death toll has been open to some debate in recent years, but appears to have been at least 128, including 77 civilians (in addition to a civilian workman later killed in the subsequent demolition of the wreckage of Beales), with some 200 more injured.

By far the worst single incident was in the Lansdowne area to the east of the Bournemouth centre. Here, the Metropole Hotel had received a direct hit. Opened almost exactly 50 years previously, this Victorian building was being used as a location for RCAF airmen as a part of the local reception centre for Canadian personnel. A large number of Canadians, in addition

Before, at the time, and after. The most prominent building that was destroyed during the 23 May 1943 raid on Bournemouth by Fw 190s of SKG 10 was the Metropole Hotel in the Lansdowne area of the town. Opened in 1893, the Metropole was one of Bournemouth's most distinctive and well-known buildings. It received a direct hit during the 23 May raid, the bomb causing the damage shown, and killing many Commonwealth servicemen. The devastation at the Metropole well illustrates the kind of significant damage an Fw 190 hit and run attack could cause. The Metropole site subsequently lay derelict until the late 1950s, when the typical late 1950s/early 1960s Royal London House was built on the site. It remains there to this day (*Bournemouth Daily Echo and Malcolm V Lowe*)

to other nationalities, were just having their Sunday lunch as the raid commenced, and most of the military casualties on that day were at the Metropole.

If SKG 10's intentions for the raid had been to strike at the town for its role in receiving and processing Allied personnel from overseas, then the objective had certainly been achieved. However, just how far the destruction of the Metropole was down to fortune or deliberate bomb-aiming is impossible to tell. At the comparatively high speed of the attackers, and their low-altitude, accurate bomb aiming against a specific building, even for skilled and experienced pilots, was a difficult task.

The raids carried out against the south coast of England by the *Jabo* Fw 190s were certainly at best a nuisance, and in cases such as the Bournemouth attack, could be deadly affairs for the local population. They tied up considerable military resources in defending against them – resources that could otherwise have been used elsewhere – and they caused great damage and destruction to life and property when they were successfully carried out. The Bournemouth attack was a classic example of what was – for the Germans – a highly successful hit and run raid.

Later in 1943 SKG 10 was reorganised, with its headquarters elements being redesignated *Stab./*SG 10 during October 1943. This was a part of a further reorganisation of the Luftwaffe's attack elements, and was subsequently to see Fw 190 ground attack and fighter-bomber units closely working with, and in some cases replacing, the increasingly vulnerable Ju 87 Stuka.

CHAPTER 12

FOREIGN OPERATORS

DESPITE THE INCREASINGLY pressing requirements that were placed on Germany's aviation industry during World War 2, a surprising number of German aircraft were exported during the war to 'friendly' or associated countries and regimes. This was to some extent the case with the Fw 190, and eventually the type served with various 'export' countries including Turkey, Rumania and Hungary. In service with the latter, the Fw 190 saw comparatively substantial frontline operational use.

Initial deliveries of Fw 190s to the Hungarian air force (the *Magyar Királyi Honvéd Légier* [MKHL], or Royal Hungarian National Air Force) began during 1944. Hungary had become an ally of the Germans partly through shared resentment against the peace treaties that followed World War 1, and eventually sided militarily with the Germans in their war against the Soviet Union, which began in 1941. Thus, the MKHL found itself fighting the Russians alongside Luftwaffe units, and Hungary became a major beneficiary of German-supplied combat aircraft of various types during the war. Eventually, some 72 Fw 190F-8 models were supplied.

It seems almost unbelievable that even bearing in mind the increasingly difficult and fragmented nature of aircraft production, repair and refurbishment in Germany in late 1944/early 1945, Fw 190s were still being supplied to Hungary during the early months of 1945. There is some disagreement amongst Hungarian sources as to which frontline MKHL units flew these aircraft in combat, it appearing likely that both 102/1 and 102/2 fighter-bomber squadrons actually used them in anger exclusively in the ground attack role. Hungarian air force combat units remained in action until late April 1945, when a lack of petrol and the deteriorating war situation put a stop to further operations.

Another of Germany's World War 2 allies, Rumania, also received a number of Fw 190s. Precise details of these aircraft remain sketchy, although it appears that they were Fw 190F models, and there could have been as many as 22 in Rumanian service. In August 1944 the Rumanians switched sides, and the fate of their Fw 190s subsequent to this remains unknown.

The largest foreign recipient of the Fw 190 could well have been Turkey, with at least 60 and possibly up to 75, plus spare parts, being supplied by the Germans during 1942-43. Turkey was one of the few countries in Europe that managed to remain neutral during World War 2, its neutrality having been formally recognised by Germany, although the Turks had also concluded agreements with Britain. Thus the Turks were supplied with arms by both sides during the conflict, and this included their new Fw 190s – all A-3 models.

In Turkish air force (*Türk Hava Kuvvetleri*) service the Fw 190s operated within elements of the 5th Air Regiment. They received the German designation Fw 190Aa-3, and were fitted with armament similar to the original Fw 190A-1 series. In a bizarre irony of war, they served in Turkey alongside British-supplied Spitfires and other British and American aircraft types.

One of the many production locations proposed for the Fw 190 was situated in France. The site for this planned manufacture was at a production facility at Cravant, which eventually came under the auspices of SNCAC. Located south-east of Paris between Auxerre and Avallon, near to the ancient village of Cravant, the SNCAC plant had some underground capacity, and also appears to have been used by Focke-Wulf as a repair and refurbishment centre. In the event, this plan did not achieve the intended results, and as in some other French establishments that were pressed into service by the Germans,

Turkey was one of a limited number of export customers for the Fw 190. Some 72 to 75 Fw 190Aa-3s were supplied in late 1942/early 1943 for *Türk Hava Kuvvetleri* service, where they operated alongside British-supplied Spitfires. As seen in this view, some did not have the standard Fw 190A-3 armament of wing-root mounted MG 151 cannons (*via R L Ward*)

the reluctance of the local workforce to support the project was a major (though not the only) stumbling block. However, the liberation of this plant by the Allies later in 1944 eventually resulted in limited production being initiated for the reborn *Armée de l'Air*.

Most French sources agree that 64 French-built Fw 190s were completed, these aircraft initially being designated AACr 6. It is possible that the description AAC 6 might also have been used. The designation was later changed to NC 900. In French service, some appear to have briefly served in the *Groupe de Chasse* GC III/5 'Normandie-Niemen', which had previously operated on the Eastern Front with the Soviet air force flying Russian-supplied fighters. Other French units that briefly employed the AACr 6/NC 900 were several CIC training units, for example at Cazaux. A communications/liaison unit at Paris/Le Bourget also appears to have briefly used the type.

The French-built Fw 190s were roughly equivalent to the Fw 190A-5 and A-8, and it seems likely that the initial aircraft produced in early 1945 were Fw 190A-5 lookalikes. There is some speculation that a number of these aircraft were made from refurbished rather than newly-made components. It has also been suggested that a second production line was projected, at Colombes, but this plan never materialised. In French service, the NC 900 did not persist for very long, as newer and more reliable types soon started to become available.

An example of the Fw 190 was supplied to Japan for trials and evaluation, this being an Fw 190A-5 lookalike. It is believed to be the only example of the Fw 190 to reach Japan, but the

A production run of 64 Fw 190A-5/A-8s was completed in a French production centre after the liberation of France as the AACr 6/NC 900. One of these rare machines survives, and is seen here painted in inappropriate German markings within the then new facilities of the *Musée de l'Air* at Le Bourget in 1975. NC 900 No 62, from the production line at Cravant, boasts a mixture of Fw 190A-5 and A-8 features (*R L Ward*)

A variety of captured Fw 190s flew in British colours and markings for evaluation purposes during and after World War 2. In the immediate aftermath of the war, several of the large number of Fw 190s that were lying around on former Luftwaffe airfields became 'unofficial' charges of operational Allied units. An example was Fw 190 EB-? (almost certainly an Fw 190F-8), which found its way into the inventory of No 41 Sqn, an RAF Spitfire operator stationed at Kastrup (Copenhagen), in Denmark

A growing number of Fw 190s fell into American hands as the war progressed, starting in North Africa and the Mediterranean theatre. Captured in the spring of 1943, this Mediterranean-theatre Fw 190 wears prominent US markings to reduce the risk of a 'friendly fire' shoot-down (*both photographs via R L Ward*)

Allies were sufficiently concerned about the possibility of the Fw 190 becoming operational with the Japanese that the Allied code name 'Fred' was assigned to the type.

Increasing numbers of Fw 190s fell into Allied hands as World War 2 progressed, commencing with the Fw 190A-3 of Arnim Faber in June 1942. In addition to the highly important evaluation that was carried out by the British on the handful of Fw 190s that landed in error in the UK, a steady flow of aircraft started to reach the Allies as Axis-controlled areas began to fall in several theatres of the war. This process commenced in North Africa, and continued following D-Day as the advancing Allied armies captured air bases used by Fw 190 units. Eventually, a large number of Fw 190s of most operational types were in Allied hands as the war drew to a close, and this number

One of the most flamboyantly marked of the captured Fw 190s was the machine that the 404th Fighter Group, Ninth Air Force, acquired at St Trond, in Belgium. Believed to be Fw 190A-8 W.Nr. 681437 (but possibly an Fw 190F-8), the aircraft came down during the Luftwaffe's mass attack on Allied airfields in north-west Europe on 1 January 1945 (Operation *Bodenplatte*). Repaired, it was painted orange-red overall, with large US national insignia, tail serial 1-1-45 and the codes OO-L (OO for the Belgian civil national identification letters and L for Leo Moon, the 404th's commander). Despite being fully repainted, the Fw 190 never flew with the 404th, however, being left behind as the unit moved on to another airfield (*John Batchelor Archive*)

increased significantly following the capitulation of Germany in May 1945. A handful of complete Ta 152s were also captured, and these proved to be of considerable interest to the Allies.

Several Fw 190s were shipped to the United States for evaluation both during and after the war. A variety of captured Fw 190s also found their way – officially or unofficially – into the inventories of some operational USAAF fighter groups. These were aircraft that were captured in the field, and were taken on by USAAF units arriving to be stationed at former Fw 190 air bases. They were most definitely not put into front line service, but were employed for familiarisation purposes, or simply as 'hacks' or for joy-rides. Many were gaudily repainted to avoid the obvious dangers of misidentification.

In a similar fashion, increasing numbers of Fw 190s also fell into Soviet hands as the war entered its final stages, Soviet forces overrunning both Luftwaffe air bases and production centres in the east in the same way as the Allies were able to in the west. In contrast to the British and Americans, however, there is evidence that Soviet air force units actually employed later model Fw 190s in combat against their former owners.

Finally, several Fw 190s accidentally landed in neutral Sweden during the course of the war, and it is believed that at least one of these was briefly flown by the Swedes presumably for evaluation purposes.

CHAPTER 13 | THE BITTER END

The victorious Allies were keen to evaluate, and where possible, use captured German technology at the end of World War 2, and one manifestation of this was the gathering of former Luftwaffe aircraft at the Royal Aircraft Establishment, Farnborough, in southern England. Here, and at other locations, a considerable amount of important evaluation and test flying duly took place. In late October and early November 1945, a selection of the captured German aircraft that had been moved to Britain for evaluation was put on display at Farnborough for the general public to inspect. Included was one of the unusual *Mistel* composite aircraft. A *Mistel* S3A, it comprised Ju 88A W.Nr. 2492 ('Air Min 77') and Fw 190A-8 W.Nr. 733759 (*Aeroplane*)

ABOVE The famous captured German Aircraft Exhibition at Farnborough in October/November 1945 contained several Fw 190s, together with this Ta 152H-1 W.Nr. 150168 ('Air Min 11') (*via Chris Ellis*)

BELOW A very large number of wrecked, destroyed, partially serviceable, serviceable and part-completed former Luftwaffe aircraft were strewn all over Europe at war's end. This Ta 152H was discovered at an unknown location, possibly Cottbus, where the type was constructed – or could this be one of the mysterious Ta 152E reconnaissance aircraft that might have been built just before the German capitulation? (*John Batchelor Archive*)

ABOVE One of several Fw 190D series aircraft that were captured by the Allies at Flensburg in Germany. This particular machine stands with several other former Luftwaffe Fw 190s, and wears an American star insignia applied to its fuselage side (*via M D Howley/R L Ward*)

ABOVE A group of Czech civilians examine abandoned and unserviceable Fw 190F-8 W.Nr. 588717 of *Stab* II./SG 2. The location is Milovice in the Protectorate of Bohemia and Moravia. On 8 May 1945 a number of aircraft from SG 2, including the wing's commander, Hans-Ulrich Rudel, fled their bases in the Czech lands to escape the advancing Russians. Some of the aircraft involved, including Rudel in his Ju 87, succeeded in reaching Kitzingen in southern Germany, where the 405th Fighter Group of the Ninth Air Force was in residence (*via R L Ward*)

BELOW Fw 190F-8/R1 W.Nr. 580434 of II./SG 4, wrecked at Hradec Králové airfield in the German-created Protectorate of Bohemia and Moravia at the end of the war. The former state of Czechoslovakia was reborn soon afterwards. The distinctive hangars in the background exist at this airfield to this day (*via Lubomír Hodan*)

BELOW A rare view of a two-seat Fw 190 wearing unit markings. The aircraft, 'red 41', is seen at the severely damaged airfield of Plzen-Bory, in the Protectorate of Bohemia and Moravia, following a devastating air raid by American bombers in April 1945 (*via Lubomír Hodan*)

ABOVE Wrecks such as this neatly belly-landed late-model Fw 190 tended to be the victim of souvenir hunters at the end of the war, although some aircraft were stripped of more usable items by the local population (*via R L Ward*)

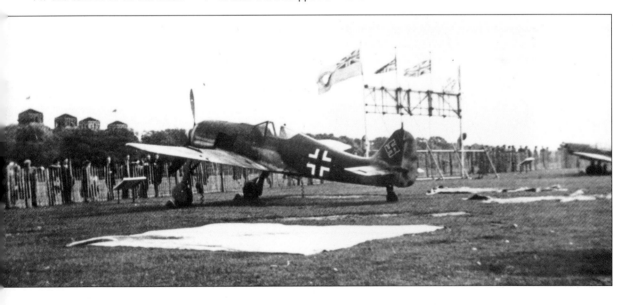

ABOVE It was not just at Farnborough that captured German aircraft were put on display for public and professionals following the end of the war. This unidentified Fw 190A or F-series aircraft was displayed at an exhibition held in London's Hyde Park in September 1945 during 'Thanksgiving Week' (*John Batchelor Archive*)

CHAPTER 14

BACK INTO PRODUCTION

THE PRODUCTION HISTORY of most of the major combat aircraft of World War 2 ends at or around the conclusion of that conflict. Few continued in widespread production for any length of time following the end of the war, as jet engine technology began to come into its own and new designs from the victors started to appear in the post-war era. Such was of course particularly true for the products of the German aircraft industry – the end of the war completely ended all remaining manufacture in Germany of the production fighters and bombers that saw frontline Luftwaffe service during the war. However, almost unique amongst the mass-produced fighters of any country from that period, the Fw 190 in the early years of the 21st century can actually be said to have returned to the production line.

The company involved in this significant and unusual project is Flug Werk GmbH of Gammelsdorf, north-east of Munich in southern Germany. Created in 1995-96, this company set out to specialise in the manufacture of components for existing historic aircraft and in specific restoration projects, but the cornerstone of its work became the new-build of brand new airworthy examples of historic aircraft. In the case of the Fw 190, this has not been simply the creation of replicas.

The new Fw 190s placed into production by Flug Werk were constructed very closely from some original drawings of the Fw 190A-8, in addition to the exact copying of surviving genuine Fw 190 parts. Initially, ambitious plans existed to build 12 new aircraft, including three actually on a genuine production line and the rest as kits. Full product support was also offered to prospective customers.

Flug Werk pointed out from the start that the airframes of the new aircraft were to be as close as 95 to 98 per cent to the original, albeit much lighter due to the deletion of armament and other heavy military equipment, and the substitution of aluminium sheet for armour plating. As the BMW 801 power-plant of the original Fw 190s has been out of production for over five decades, an alternative had to be sought for the new aircraft that would match the size, shape and power output of the BMW engine. Eventually, Flug Werk decided upon the Russian Shvetsov ASh-82T or FN 14-cylinder two-row radial in its Chinese-built form as the Huosai HS-7. This engine is readily available, and has a good spares back-up as well.

The ASh-82 was one of the Soviet Union's most successful piston engines, and in its original M-82 form was the powerplant that was fitted to some of the radial-engined Lavochkin fighters that flew in combat against Fw 190s during World War 2! A number of other alterations to the original Fw 190A-8's systems and equipment were envisaged, partly to use readily available modern parts and partly to satisfy present-day airworthiness requirements. One of the alterations involved the self-sealing fuselage fuel tanks of the original Fw 190s being replaced on the Flug Werk machines by welded sheet-metal components, offering considerably greater fuel-carrying capacity. However, each of the 12 new aircraft was scheduled to be fitted with a genuine World War 2-vintage Fw 190 tail-wheel undercarriage unit – a number of these original items have seemingly found their way into the hands of Flug Werk.

Flug Werk's designation for the new Fw 190s was established as FW 190A-8/N, with the capital letters 'FW' standing for Flug Werk and the 'N' meaning *Nachbau* (literally, 'remake'). The stated price for one of the FW 190A-8/N kits in 2001 was

A genuine new-build Fw 190. Assembled on the Flug Werk production line at Gammelsdorf, near Munich, or available as a kit, the FW 190A-8/N is a very close recreation of the original Fw 190A-8, and is based where possible on original blueprints and information (*Jürgen Schelling*)

Closely resembling the Fw 190A-8, the Flug Werk FW 190A-8/N is of course unarmed, and is powered by a Chinese derivative of a long-standing Russian radial engine (*Jürgen Schelling*)

approximately $525,000. Some of the components for these new aircraft were built at various sub-contractors in Eastern Europe. At the time of writing this text in the summer of 2002, the Flug Werk project was progressing, although none of the new machines had flown at that time. Additionally, the possibility also existed that two new-build Fw 190D *Dora-9* models were under consideration for production by Flug Werk, possibly using the Rolls-Royce Griffon engine as their power-plant. It was also envisaged that one of the FW 190A-8/N kits would be completed as a two-seater to allow conversion and familiarisation training for prospective clients.

With production having thus recommenced of new and civilianised Fw 190s, in many ways it is fitting that the story of Focke-Wulf's legendary fighter is continuing in this way. The Fw 190 was a great aircraft, and its spirit will live on for a long time yet.

APPENDICES

PRINCIPAL AIRCRAFT PLANTS INVOLVED IN Fw 190 AND Ta 152 PRODUCTION

The production effort involved in producing some 20,000+ Fw 190s was enormous, and sadly some of the key documentation relating to this process has never surfaced to allow historians to compile a definitive list of Fw 190 producers. The following is a tentative list of aircraft manufacturers known to have been involved in Fw 190 production or recycling. In addition to these, it must be remembered that there were many smaller plants, supplying components and carrying out repairs to badly damaged airframes, that do not feature in these summaries as they were not builders of the completed airframes.

Fw 190 AND Ta 152 PRINCIPAL MANUFACTURERS INCLUDED:

Focke-Wulf plants at Bremen (and surrounding area), Marienburg (now Malbork, in Poland), Cottbus, Aslau, Posen (now Poznan, in Poland), Sorau and various other locations. Arado at Warnemünde and Tutow.

AGO at Oschersleben and dispersed sites.
Fieseler at Kassel (two major plants).
Mimetall (Mitteldeutsche Metallwerke GmbH) at Erfurt.
Weser at several locations including Nordenham.
Arbeits-Gemeinschaft Roland at Leipzig and possibly other locations.
ATG (Allegemeine Transportanlage GmbH) at Leipzig.
Norddeutsche Dornier at Wismar.

Various other locations were planned for Fw 190 or Ta 152 production, including the REIMAHG underground facility at Kahla, near Jena (REIMAHG was later switched to Me 262 production). Many other organisations such as Erla at Leipzig, Siebel at Halle and other locations, the airline Deutsche Lufthansa at various locations, the Gothaer Waggonfabrik at Gotha and so on were involved in producing components, complete aircraft, performing major repairs, or would have built later models of the Fw 190 and/or Ta 152 if World War 2 had continued.

Fw 190 AND Ta 152 *WERK NUMMERN*

It has been a preoccupation of serious historians for many years to attempt to piece together a complete list of Fw 190 *Werk Nummern*. Unfortunately, so far this task has eluded even the most diligent researcher. The lack of complete documentary evidence, the existence of conflicting information, the number of different factories involved in Fw 190 production and the rebuilding or recycling of existing airframes into new models are just some of the reasons why a complete list of *Werk Nummern* does not currently exist – and may indeed never do so. A consequence of this, as previously related, is the impossibility of working out a precise overall production total for the Fw 190.

It is very interesting to note the extremely wide variance on this subject between published sources, with rarely any agreement in published accounts – even between those that claim to have all the answers! The less than precise or accurate translations of some German-language publications into English has similarly helped to confuse the issue amongst some published sources.

The following is offered as the most complete listing known to the Author at the present time, and has been pieced together over a number of years where possible from original documents, and archive sources in Germany, but in many places the frustrating need to simply quote the start of a block of *Werk Nummern* instead of a complete and authenticated block remains a necessity. It will be noted that not all the numbers within a block were necessarily allocated to a specific airframe, as major gaps within identified blocks also exist.

Some of this information agrees with previouslypublished sources and some is very much at variance with other published accounts. However, regarding published sources, it is interesting to note how many writers have quoted comparatively low production totals for specific Fw 190 versions, but nevertheless conclude by saying that over 20,000 Fw 190s in total were manufactured. Yet if one adds up their production totals for specific versions, these come to nowhere near 20,000. Indeed, some fall short even of 10,000. It seems that some Fw 190 writers were not very accomplished at arithmetic!

A good example is the Fw 190A-8, which most writers recognise as being built in larger numbers than any other A-series Fw 190. The often-quoted production total for this version is around 1334 or 1344. If we take it that this model was built mainly in 1944 alongside some late model Fw 190G series, the Fw 190F-8, the early A-9 models and the F-9, plus the Fw 190D-9, nevertheless the totals quoted in many published sources for these variants combined does not come anywhere near to the 11,411 Fw 190s that appear to have been taken on strength during 1944 if the oft-quoted Luftwaffe acceptance figures for 1944 are to be believed. It is the Author's contention that in reality, the production figure for the Fw 190A-8 was probably somewhere between 2000 and 2500, and quite possibly more than that. Apart from the Fw 190A-1, where we can be very near to certain that 102 examples were built, and the Fw 190A-7, where 80 appear to have been made before production was taken over by the A-8, otherwise the same upwards assessment must surely also be applied to the often quoted production figures for other Fw 190A series versions.

There is a final footnote to Fw 190 production totals. If one considers the rebuilt and recycled Fw 190s that were made from earlier marks as rebuilds, and not as new aircraft, the final production total for the whole Fw 190 line is actually much less than 20,000. This really depends upon what one considers to be a 'new' aircraft.

Fw 190 VERSION	*WERK NUMMER* ALLOCATIONS
Fw 190A-0	0008 to 0035: manufactured at Bremen. Focke-Wulf documents usually refer to these aircraft with the prefix '190.' ahead of the numbers (e.g. 190.0015). However, W.Nr. 0006 also existed, and many development airframes from 0036 consecutively onwards were also very important to the Fw 190 programme. These were possibly from a second batch of Fw 190A-0 airframes – or were perhaps taken from the Fw 190A-1 production line?
Fw 190A-1	110001 to 110102. Sometimes quoted in documents with an additional '0' ahead of the number: production at Bremen and Marienburg.
Fw 190A-2	120201 to 120509 (again sometimes with an additional '0'): production at Bremen and Marienburg. 122051 to 122290 (again sometimes with an additional '0'): production by AGO at Oschersleben. 125191 to 125530 (again sometimes with an additional '0'): production by Arado at Warnemünde.
Fw 190A-3	130201 to 130509 (again sometimes with an additional '0'): production at Bremen and Marienburg. 32051 to 132290 or 132299 (again sometimes with an additional '0'): production by AGO at Oschersleben.

135191 to 135530 (again sometimes with an additional '0'): production by Arado at Warnemünde.
137001 to 137020 (again sometimes with an additional '0'): production by Fieseler at Kassel.

Fw 190A-4

140561 to 140810 (again sometimes with an additional '0'): production at Bremen and Marienburg.
142291 to 142520 (again sometimes with an additional '0'): production by AGO at Oschersleben.
145531 to circa 145845 (again sometimes with an additional '0'): production by Arado at Warnemünde.
147001 or 147021 to 147200 (again sometimes with an additional '0'): production by Fieseler at Kassel.

Fw 190A-5

151040 or 151041 to 151751 (again sometimes with an additional '0'): production at Bremen and particularly Marienburg. Might also have had an additional '0' added after the initial '15'; possibly also included the block circa 150168 to 150585.
152521 to 152746 (again sometimes with an additional '0'): production by AGO at Oschersleben.
155845 to 156024 or 156025 (again sometimes with an additional '0'): production by Arado at Warnemünde.
157201 to 157375 (again sometimes with an additional '0'): block might have continued to 157401, or renumbered from 710001: production by Fieseler at Kassel.
410001 to 410275: production by AGO at Oschersleben.
150811 to 150959 (again sometimes with an additional '0'): production possibly by Focke-Wulf at Sorau, although the Sorau factory might not have been ready for production at that time.
This is also the first Fw 190 A-series version where *Werk Nummer* allocations to unidentified locations have been identified, including 840001 to 840205, and 680001 to 680205.

Fw 190A-6

470001 to 470085, 470201 to 470270 or 470275, 470401 to 470485, 470581 to 470650 or 470655, and 470745 to

470800 or 470801: production by Arado at Warnemünde.
530101 to 530150, 530301 to 530430 or 530431, 530711 to 530770 or 530771, 530901 to 530960 or 530961, 531051 or 531151 to 531110 or 531210: production by Fieseler at Kassel.
550130 to 550220, 550420 to 550575, 550710 to 550800, 550870 to 550930, 551095 to 551145 (numbering of final block unconfirmed): production by AGO at Oschersleben.
650315 to 650510: another mystery block, possibly made by Focke-Wulf at Sorau or Arado at Warnemünde.

Fw 190A-7

340001 to 340085, 340210 to 340360: production by Focke-Wulf at Cottbus, although few made as A-7 model.
430160 to 430200, 430310 to 430370, 430460 to 430510, 430640 to 430710, 430990 to 430999, 431001 to 431020, 431110 to 431190 or circa 431195: production by AGO at Oschersleben, increasingly at dispersed locations due to Allied bombing, although few made as A-7 model.
642001 to 642016, 642520 to 642560, 642960 to 642999, 643401 to 643420, 643701 to 643730, 643901 to 643950: production by Fieseler at Kassel, although few made as A-7 model.

Fw 190A-8

170001 to 170140, 170301 to 170450, 170601 to 170750, 170901 to 171100, 171151 to 171200, 171450 to 171750, 172340 to 172360, 172601 to 172750, 172910 to 172999, 173001 to 173100, 173801 to 173950, 174001 to 174050, 174100 to 174135, 175001 to 175300, 175901 to 175990, 176001 to 176200, 177001 to 177610 (possibly the latter was simply a completion block of 20 machines): production by Focke-Wulf at Cottbus.
350151 to 350300, 350851 to 350875: production by Focke-Wulf at Aslau.
352501 to 352520, 620001 to circa 620205: production by Weser.
380151 to 380180, 380320 to 380410: production by Arado at Tutow.
680101 to 680200, 680410 to 680600, 680710 to 680860, 680930 to 680970, 681020 to 681050, 681250 to 681540,

681801 to 681900, 681960 to 681999, 682001 to 682070, 682170 to 682320, 682640 to 682840, 682901 to 682999, 683310 to 683340: production by Fieseler at Kassel.

730280 to 730520, 730880 to 730999, 731001 to 731120, 731390 to 731480, 731710 to 731810, 731980 to 731999, 732001 to 732310, 733670 to 733790, 733960 to 733999, 734001 to 734040, 734350 to 734400, 737340 to 737440, 737920 to 737999, 738100 to 738399 or 738400, 739130 to 739580, 739620 to 739640: production by AGO at Oschersleben in several dispersed locations.

960201 to 960330, 960450 to 960560, 960640 to circa 960899, 961050 to 961250, 961601 to 961700, 961930 to 961970: production by Norddeutsche Dornier at Wismar.

Several unidentified Fw 190A-8 blocks also exist, including 690101 to 690160 (possibly built by Fieseler) and 960001 to 960110 (possibly Norddeutsche Dornier's opening production batch).

Fw 190A-9	202125 to circa 202319, 202360 to 202450, 202565 to 202590, 205001 to 205100, 205180 to 205300, 205901 to 205999, 206031 to 206200, 207160 to circa 207240, 208378 to circa 209915: production by Focke-Wulf at Cottbus. 490020 to 490050: production by Focke-Wulf at Aslau. 750070 to 750160: production by Mimetall at Erfurt. 980150 to 980230, 980360 to 980380, 980540 to 980590: production by Norddeutsche Dornier at Wismar. Again, there are several unidentified blocks of numbers for the A-9, including 380001 onwards.
Fw 190D-9	210001 to 210300: production/ conversion by Focke-Wulf, Cottbus and Langenhagen. 210901 to 210999, 211001 to 211200, 211901 to 211950, 212101 to 212170: production/conversion by Focke-Wulf, Cottbus. This location possibly also responsible for 213201 to 213299. 400201 to 400320, 600121 to 600180, 600311 to 600450, 600630 to 600670, 600761 to 600810, 600980 to 601110,

601301 to 601350, 601410 to 601480, 601961 to 601980: production/conversion by Fieseler at Kassel. 401351 to 401400: production/conversion by Norddeutsche Dornier at Wismar. 500001 to 500100, 500381 to 500440, 500551 to 500650: production/conversion by Mimetall at Erfurt. Several unidentified blocks include 501001 to circa 501299, possibly by Weser.

Fw 190D-11	220001 to circa 220013 and probably beyond: production/conversion probably by Focke-Wulf at Langenhagen or Cottbus. Many historians do not acknowledge the existence of a D-11 production series.
Fw 190D-12	Production by both Fieseler and Arado, but *Werk Nummern* unidentified.
Fw 190D-13	836001 to circa 836030 and probably beyond: production/conversion by Arbeits-Gemeinschaft Roland at Leipzig and possibly other locations.
Fw 190F-1	Many Fw 190F-1s were redesignated from Fw 190A-4/U3s. However, an allocation 610001 to circa 610030 has been rumoured for many years. This is possibly the block of F-1 aircraft actually built as that, although if it was, the manufacturer is as yet unidentified.
Fw 190F-2	Many Fw 190F-2s were redesignated from Fw 190A-5/U3s. However, production of actual Fw 190F-2 is believed to have taken place by Focke-Wulf at Sorau (possibly within the block 180001 onwards), and by AGO at Oschersleben (possibly within the block 410001 onwards, this being an Fw 190A-5 block allocation).
Fw 190F-3	670001 to 671150: production by Arado at Warnemünde.
Fw 190F-8	Production/conversion by Arado at Warnemünde, in the following

blocks: 421001 onwards (possibly), 424001 onwards, 425001 onwards, 426001 onwards, 428001 onwards, 580001 onwards, 581001 onwards, 582001 onwards, 583001 onwards, 584001 onwards, 585001 onwards, 586001 onwards, 587001 onwards, 588001 onwards, 589001 onwards, and possibly 593001 onwards. Production/conversion by Norddeutsche Dornier at Wismar in the following blocks: 930001 to 930838, 931001 onwards, 932001 onwards, and 933001 onwards. Also possibly production/conversion by AGO at Oschersleben and dispersed sites. Many allocated blocks remain unidentified to a particular manufacturer.

Fw 190F-9 Production/conversion mainly by Arado at Warnemünde in the following blocks: 420101 onwards, 424001 onwards, 426001 onwards, 580001 onwards, 583001 onwards, and 586001 onwards. Some of these are Fw 190F-8 blocks, numbers being allocated to either F-8 or F-9 from these blocks. Again, several allocated blocks of numbers are unaccounted for, and the manufacturer of the following is unidentified (possibly Norddeutsche Dornier): 428001 to 428460, 440001 or 440121 to 440580, and 445001 onwards.

Fw 190G-1 Many Fw 190G-1s were redesignated from Fw 190A-4/U8s. A new-build Fw 190G-1 batch appears to have been made, but no details of block allocations have yet come to light.

Fw 190G-2 Many Fw 190G-2s were redesignated from Fw 190A-5/U8s. However, production of actual Fw 190G-2s is believed to have taken place either by Focke-Wulf at Sorau or by AGO at Oschersleben (possibly within the block 161001 onwards, or 180941 onwards).

Fw 190G-3 Production possibly by Arado at Warnemünde within the block 160001 onwards, and possibly 110001 onwards (a different block to the

Fw 190A-1! A block with similar numbers was also allocated for several Ta 152 *Versuchs* aircraft from Sorau and Adelheide).

Fw 190G-8 Production/conversion possibly by Arado at Warnemünde or Norddeutsche Dornier at Wismar within block 190001 to circa 190450.

Fw 190S-5/S-8 Two-seat conversion trainer derived from Fw 190A-5 and A-8/U1 conversions. Apparently a conversion-only programme mainly in the field at locations such as the Altenburg training airfield.

Ta 152V series A series of development aircraft was planned from Sorau and Adelheide for the Ta 152 programme, but many were not built. *Werk Nummern* were from 110001 onwards, but 110006 was apparently the first number used.

Ta 152C-1 Production commenced by Siebel at Halle-Schkeuditz in the block 360001 onwards, and by Allegemein Transportanlage at Leipzig in the block 920001 onwards.

Ta 152E-1 Production commenced by Mimetall at Erfurt (actually Erfurt-North), *Werk Nummern* unknown.

Ta 152H-0 150001 to 150020: production by Focke-Wulf at Cottbus.

Ta 152H-1 150021 to 150040, 150167 to 150169: production by Focke-Wulf at Cottbus. Many more H-series planned but not built, although possibly one Ta 152H-2 built at Cottbus.

NC 900 01 to 64. Built in France at Cravant, near Auxerre, under the auspices of SNCAC. Originally designated AACr 6, also possibly AAC 6. Roughly equivalent to Fw 190A-5 and A-8.

NOTE

Particular thanks during the compiling of this section to Peter Walter, especially for his persistence in finally obtaining copies from German archives of various Focke-Wulf *Produktionsübersichten* documents. Thank you also to Andrew Arthy

CODE SYSTEM FOR GERMAN AIRCRAFT MANUFACTURERS

It is an established and widely used practice in many industries for manufacturers to identify themselves on their products, and to specify their serial or works number. This is often accomplished by means of a small metal manufacturers' plate attached to the component or complete product in a prominent or sometimes hidden location. Aircraft manufacturers and their component suppliers are no exception in this, and German aircraft companies continued the practice even well into World War 2. Due to this, captured German aircraft tended to give much useful data about themselves to their new owners, once the relevant makers' plates had been discovered and read.

There is no doubt that several factories found themselves on the list of targets for Allied bombers due to such information being contained on their products, this source of information being a useful addition to the Allies' overall intelligence effort to identify targets in the German aircraft industry. Growing concern within the RLM, the Luftwaffe and the aircraft industry in general eventually resulted in moves to end this highly informative practice, and generally from 1942 onwards (but with exceptions) a new system was introduced in which three-digit codes were used on simplified manufacturers' plates. Just where the official sanction came from for this new system is not easy to determine. However, it did begin to arise at around the time that *Werk Nummer* sequences were being deliberately changed on RLM insistence also for security reasons.

The three-digit codes identified the manufacturer of the aircraft to those in the know, but not to the Allies. It was intended that these codes would be written in lower case lettering. However, this was not necessarily the case on the plates themselves. An example is the manufacturer's plate discovered within the fuselage of the preserved Fw 190F-8 W.Nr. 931884, which is part of the National Air and Space Museum (NASM) in the United States.

During the complete restoration of this aircraft in the early 1980s, the manufacturer's plate found in the aircraft's fuselage contained the three-digit manufacturer's code HKZ stamped in capital letters. This fuselage had originally been part of Fw 190 W.Nr. 640069 built by Arado at Warnemünde. It was almost certainly an Fw 190A-7. The fuselage of this aircraft, including its manufacturer's data plate, was then incorporated into the parts that were subsequently made up as Fw 190F-8 W.Nr. 931884 – yet another example of one Fw 190 being re-cycled into another. The exact location where W.Nr. 931884 was fabricated, incidentally, is open to debate.

Research by the NASM at the time of the aircraft's restoration suggested that the work was performed by Arado at Warnemünde, but it now seems more likely that it was put together by Norddeutsche Dornier at Wismar. It took the NASM, incidentally, just over three years – and 13,604 man hours – to completely restore this historic aircraft to static display condition.

The three-digit factory codes that have so far been identified as relating to aircraft companies, and locations, associated with Fw 190 production are identified below. This data is presented with the usual proviso that the list contains the most up to date information so far available, and that documentation that does exist appears to confirm these codes and locations:

Focke-Wulf, Bremen	gwy
Focke-Wulf, Adelheide	naw
Focke-Wulf, Cottbus	naz
Focke-Wulf, Marienburg	nat
Focke-Wulf, Posen	nba
Focke-Wulf, Sorau	ncc
AGO, Oschersleben	jhe
Arado, Warnemünde	hkz
Dornier, Wismar	hmw
Erla, Leipzig	mcu
Fieseler, Kassel	hps
Siebel, Halle/Saale	jbn
Weser, Berlin-Tempelhof	mdk
Weser, Nordenham	mdl

SELECTED Fw 190 SPECIFICATIONS

Data in this section has been derived from Focke-Wulf's own figures where possible, or from data obtained from aircraft captured by the Allies. The empty weight is taken to include the aircraft's internal armament, but not ammunition. As pointed out elsewhere, various different armament options were open to most marks of Fw 190, only the basic internal armament is included here. The engine power rating is for maximum power at take-off.

It will be noted that the dimensions quoted here, particularly for the wingspan and length, do not tally with some published sources. This is because there are about as many different variations on Fw 190 dimensions as there are published specifications. The data contained in this book is taken, where possible, directly from original Focke-Wulf documentation, including the official Aircraft Handbook for the Fw 190A-8 D.(*Luft*)T.2190A-8. This document was issued to units operating the Fw 190A-8, and one would expect it to contain correct figures. The wingspan quoted, unequivocally, and in several places in this handbook, is 10,500 mm (i.e. 10.50 m).

However, unfortunately Focke-Wulf themselves were less than helpful on this score, as some other surviving company drawings certainly quote slightly different dimensions – although these appear to refer to design proposals, and not actual production installations. Similarly, figures such as 10.49 m and 10.506 m also tend to be published regularly for the wingspan of the Fw 190A series (and also 10.383 m for some of the earlier A-series models).

It is the Author's belief that the discrepancy in some published sources has come about due to conversions made into feet and inches, and vice versa. However, 10.506 m also has its passionate adherents, which is duly acknowledged here. An interesting point is that most German historians now accept the wingspan of the A-model Fw 190 as 10.50 m, while many British historians accept 10.506 m. The sometimes-quoted 10.49 m does not appear on any Focke-Wulf drawings that the Author has ever seen. Similarly, the sometimes used 10.51 m is perhaps a rounding-up of 10.506 m. Another possible explanation for increased span in some sources is the clear cover over the Fw 190's wingtip navigation lights, which could have been taken to have added several millimetres to the overall wingspan. The same problem exists over the fuselage length of the A-model Fw 190. Again, there are many variations between published sources. The figures quoted in this book for fuselage dimensions are those most often seen on Focke-Wulf's own documentation, and are also the figures that most German historians now agree upon.

Fw 190A-8

Span	10.50 m
Length	8.95 m
Height	3.95 m
Wing Area	18.30 m sq
Empty Weight	3490 kg
Loaded Weight	4440 kg
Max Speed	647 km/h at 5500 m
Ceiling	10,300 m
Powerplant	BMW 801D-2 of 1700 hp
Armament	2 x 13 mm Rheinmetall-Borsig MG 131 machine guns in upper forward fuselage, with up to 475 rounds per gun (rpg); 2 x 20 mm Mauser MG 151 cannons in wing-roots with 250 rpg; 2 x 20 mm Mauser MG 151 cannons in the outer wings with 140 rpg

Fw 190F-8

Span	10.50 m
Length	8.95 m
Height	3.95 m
Wing Area	18.30 m sq
Empty Weight	3323 kg
Loaded Weight	4400 kg
Max Speed	634 km/h at 5500 m
Ceiling	(reliable data unavailable)
Powerplant	BMW 801D-2 of 1700 hp
Armament	2 x 13 mm Rheinmetall-Borsig MG 131 machine-guns in upper forward fuselage, with up to 475 rpg; 2 x 20 mm Mauser MG 151 cannons in wing-roots with 250 rpg

Fw 190D-9

Span	10.50 m
Length	10.192 m
Height	3.36 m
Wing Area	18.30 sq m
Empty Weight	3490 kg
Loaded Weight	4840 kg
Max Speed	686 km/h at 6600 m
Ceiling	13,200 m
Powerplant	Junkers Jumo 213A-1 of 1770 hp
Armament	2 x 13 mm Rheinmetall-Borsig MG 131 machine guns in upper forward fuselage, with up to 475 rpg; 2 x 20 mm Mauser MG 151 cannons in wing-roots with 250 rpg

Ta 152H-1

Span	14.44 m
Length	10.710 m
Height	3.36 m
Wing Area	23.30 sq m
Empty Weight	3920 kg
Loaded Weight	5220 kg
Max Speed	718 km/h at 10,700 m
Ceiling	14,800 m
Powerplant	Junkers Jumo 213E-1 of 1750 hp
Armament	2 x 20 mm Mauser MG 151 cannons in wing-roots with 175 rpg; 1 x 30 mm Rheinmetall-Borsig MK 108 cannon engine-mounted firing through propeller spinner, with 90 rounds

GLOSSARY

AACr French Fw 190 manufacturer Ateliers Aéronautiques de Cravant

AEG the German electrical giant, which became the owner of Focke-Wulf on its becoming a GmbH

AG *Aktiengesellschaft* (roughly equivalent to a joint-stock company)

AGO various names seem to have made up this abbreviation, including Aerowerke Gustav Otto

ATG Allgemeine Transportanlage GmbH (sometimes written as Allgemeine Transportanlage Gesellschaft mbH)

BFW Bayerische Flugzeugwerke AG (sometimes also written Bayerische Flugzeug Werke AG)

BMW Bayerische Motorenwerke AG (sometimes also written Bayerische Motoren Werke AG)

CO Commanding Officer

Dipl.-Ing. *Diplom-Ingenieur* (literally a Diploma Engineer, roughly equivalent to an engineering Degree in a specific engineering subject)

FuG *Funk Gerät* (literally radio set or apparatus, the generic designation [e.g. the Lorenz FuG 7-type radio equipment in early Fw 190A models] used for radio, IFF etc. equipment in the Fw 190 and other types)

GmbH *Gesellschaft mit beschränkter Haftung* (roughly equivalent to a British Limited Company)

GM abbreviated designation for the GM-1 nitrous oxide used for boosting the power output of some German piston engines (also sometimes written in contemporary documents unhyphenated as GM 1)

IFF Identification Friend/Foe

Jabo-Rei *Jagdbomber mit vergrößerter Reichweite* (literally 'fighter-bomber with increased range', this term often being used for the Fw 190G series)

JG *Jagdgeschwader* (Luftwaffe fighter wing)

Luftflotte (Luftwaffe air fleet)

MKHL *Magyar Királyi Honvéd Légier*, or Royal Hungarian National Air Force

MW abbreviated designation for the MW-50 methanol-water used for boosting the power output of some German piston engines (also sometimes written in contemporary documents unhyphenated as MW 50)

NASM National Air and Space Museum (United States)

R *Rüstsatz* (plural, *Rüstsätze* – not *Rüstsätzen*), the conversion kits or sets (often concerned with add-on armament options) for installation in the field

Revi *Reflexvisier* (literally reflex gunsight, the generic designation for gunsights carried in some German military aircraft)

RLM *Reichsluftfahrtministerium*, the Third Reich's Aviation Ministry

RM *Reichsmark* (the unit of currency of the Third Reich)

rpg rounds per gun

SG *Schlachtgeschwader* (Luftwaffe ground attack wing)

SKG *Schnellkampfgeschwader* (Luftwaffe fast [fighter-] bomber wing)

SNCAC Société Nationale de Constructions Aéronautiques du Centre

U *Umrüst-Bausatz* (plural, *Umrüst-Bausätze*), the conversion kits or sets installed at the factory to give a particular equipment fit or capability

V *Versuchs* or *Versuchsmuster*, the term used to describe an experimental or test airframe, not a prototype

VFW Vereinigte Flugtechnische Werke GmbH

ZG *Zerstörergeschwader* (Luftwaffe [twin-engined] fighter [literally 'destroyer'] wing)

FURTHER READING

A large number of books and magazine articles have been published on the Fw 190 over the years. Some of these have been good, some not so good, but most have shed light to one extent or another on important aspects of the Fw 190's story. Many of these published sources are now long out of print. Of the English-language books that are currently available, or have been recently published, a number of these are listed below as potentially useful further reading – for information on aspects of the Fw 190's story that have not been the main focus of this book, or as a useful background to some of the issues raised.

Air War Italy 1944-45 by Nick Beale, Ferdinando D'Amico and Gabriele Valentini, Airlife Publishing, 1996

Doras of the Galland Circus: Eagle Files No 1 by Jerry Crandall, Eagle Editions, 1999

Osprey Aircraft of the Aces 6 – Focke-Wulf Fw 190 Aces of the Russian Front by John Weal, Osprey Publishing, 1995

Osprey Aircraft of the Aces 9 – Focke-Wulf Fw 190 Aces of the Western Front by John Weal, Osprey Publishing, 1996

Osprey Aviation Elite 1 – Jagdgeschwader 2 'Richthofen' by John Weal, Osprey Publishing, 2000

Osprey Aviation Elite 6 – Jagdgeschwader 54 'Grünherz' by John Weal, Osprey Publishing, 2001

Osprey Modelling Manual No 20 – Focke-Wulf Fw 190 by Rodrigo Hernandez Cabos and Geoff Coughlin, Osprey Publishing, 2002.

Focke-Wulf Fw 190 In Combat by Alfred Price, Sutton Publishing, 1998

Focke-Wulf Fw 190F/G by Alex Janda and Tomáz Poruba, JaPo, no publishing history data

Focke-Wulf Fw 190 & Ta 152: Aircraft & Legend by Heinz J Nowarra, Haynes Publishing, 1988

Focke-Wulf Ta 152 by Dietmar Hermann, Schiffer Publishing, 1999

Fw 190A/F/G/S: Aircraft Monograph No 4 by Adam Skupiewski, AJ Press/Books International, 1996

German Aircraft Industry and Production, 1933-1945 by Ferenc A Vajda and Peter Dancey, Airlife Publishing, 1998

Luftwaffe Codes, Markings and Units 1939-1945 by Barry C Rosch, Schiffer Publishing, 1995

Luftwaffe In Detail: Air War over the Czech Lands by Jiri Rajlich, Wings & Wheels Publications, 2000.

Mistel by Robert Forsyth, Classic Publications, 2001

Sturmstaffel 1 by Eric Mombeek with Robert Forsyth and Eddie J Creek, Classic Publications, 1999

The Luftwaffe Album by Joachim Dressel and Manfred Griehl, Arms and Armour Press/Cassell, 1997

The Luftwaffe Data Book by Alfred Price, Greenhill Books, 1997

War Prizes by Phil Butler, Midland Counties Publications, 1994

Wings of the Luftwaffe by Captain Eric Brown, Macdonald and Jane's/Pilot Press, 1977

World War 2 Luftwaffe Fighter Modelling by Geoff Coughlin, Osprey Publishing, 2000

SELECTED WEB SITES

There are many web sites that deal with the Fw 190. Like published sources, some are infinitely better than others. The following are a number of the more interesting, which again cover aspects of the Fw 190's story in greater background detail than is possible in this book, or link to other interesting sites. Some of these sites refer to the Fw 190 as a part of their overall coverage.

http://www.focke-wulf190.de
http://www.geocities.com/bookie190
http://www.luftwaffe.cz
http://www.warbirdsresourcegroup.org/LRG
http://www.ww2.dk

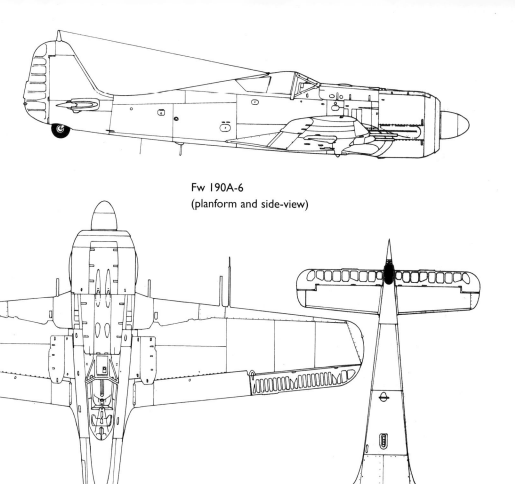

Fw 190A-6
(planform and side-view)

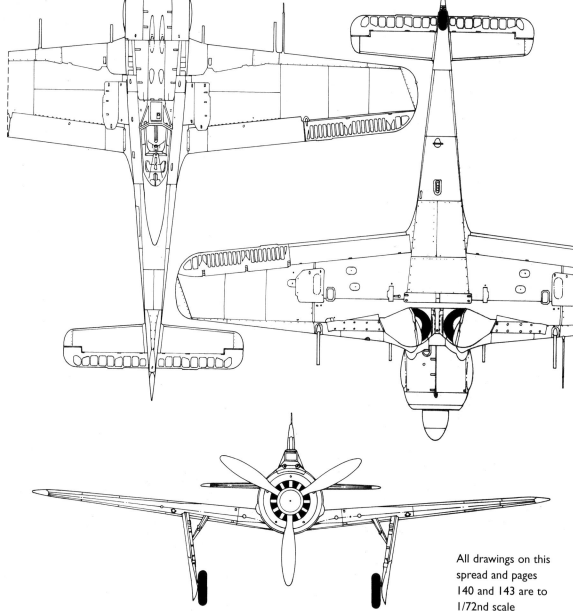

All drawings on this
spread and pages
140 and 143 are to
1/72nd scale

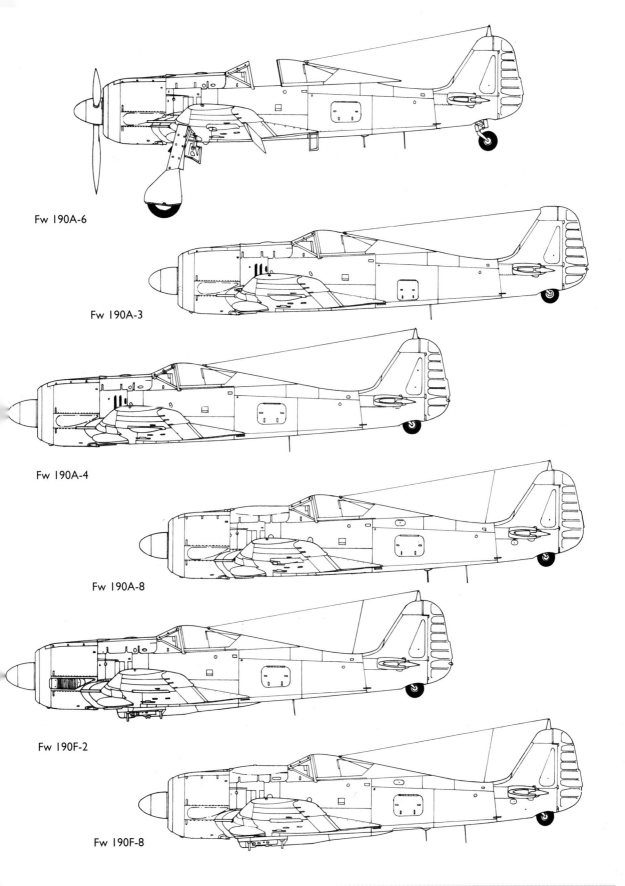

Fw 190A-6

Fw 190A-3

Fw 190A-4

Fw 190A-8

Fw 190F-2

Fw 190F-8

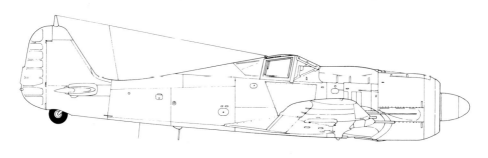

Fw 190A-8/R8 *Sturm*
(planform and side-view)

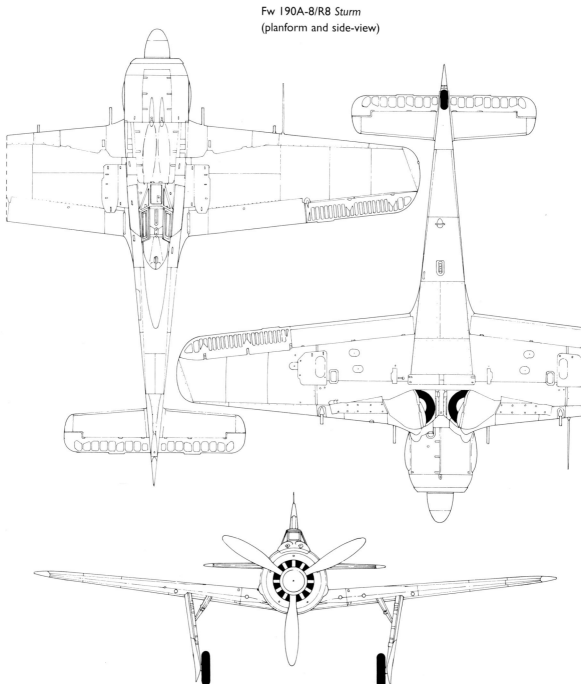

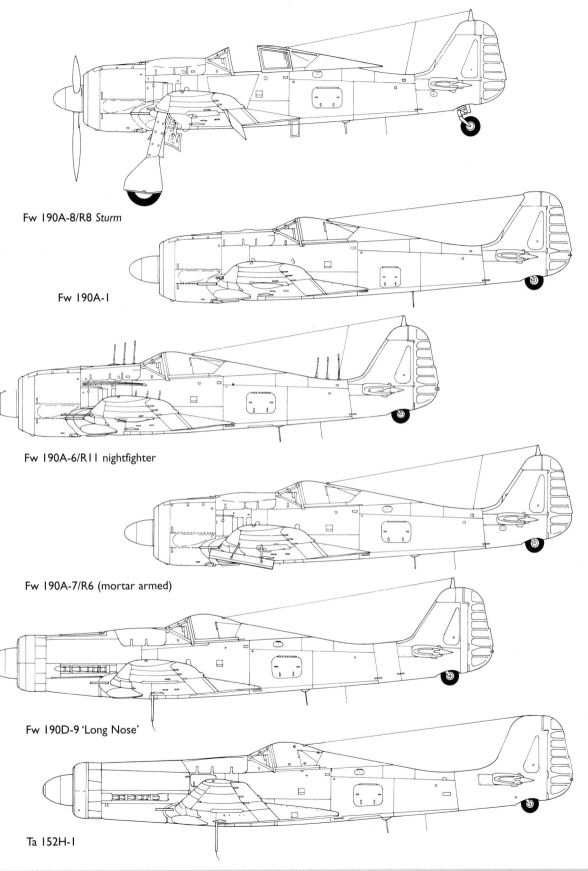

Fw 190A-8/R8 *Sturm*

Fw 190A-1

Fw 190A-6/R11 nightfighter

Fw 190A-7/R6 (mortar armed)

Fw 190D-9 'Long Nose'

Ta 152H-1

INDEX

Figures in **bold** refer to illustrations